Economic Thought in Islam

A Study of Alinomics

Economic Thought in Islam

A Study of Alinomics

Dr. Sayed Afzal Peerzade
Chairperson, Department of Economics,
Karnataka State Women's University,
Bijapur, Karnataka

New Century Publications
New Delhi, India

NEW CENTURY PUBLICATIONS
4800/24, Bharat Ram Road,
Ansari Road, Daryaganj,
New Delhi - 110 002 (India)

Tel.: 011-2324 7798, 4358 7398, 6539 6605
Fax: 011-4101 7798
E-mail: indiatax@vsnl.com • info@newcenturypublications.com
www.newcenturypublications.com

Editorial office:
LG-7, Aakarshan Bhawan,
4754-57/23, Ansari Road, Daryaganj,
New Delhi - 110 002

Tel.: 011-4356 0919

First Published: **2014**

ISBN: **978-81-7708-369-9**

Published by New Century Publications and printed at Salasar Imaging Systems, New Delhi.

Designs: Patch Creative Unit, New Delhi.

PRINTED IN INDIA

This Work is Dedicated to My Mother

Amat'ur Rauf Hashmi

(d. 1987)

About Book

In the last few decades, a lot of interest has been generated in the study of economic thought in Islam. In spite of several works published on the subject, not much has been written on economic ideas of Ali, who was one of the most prominent caliphs (deputies) of the Prophet of Islam. Not much is known on the economic, political and administrative policies Ali pursued and moral values he upheld even in the most trying circumstances.

The present work attempts to fill this vacuum. A dispassionate study of the economic ideas of Ali makes it clear that he was a distinct precursor to several economic values, which continue to dominate even today, the mainstream economic thinking worldwide. He excelled, in both letter and spirit, to solve whenever a new economic problem confronted him. The justification, which Ali provided, was amazingly incredible and never heard before. His ideas may be rightly termed as *Alinomics*.

About the Author

Dr. Sayed Afzal Peerzade (b. 1954) is Chairperson, Department of Economics, Karnataka State Women's University, Bijapur, Karnataka, since 2003-04. He has published the following books: *Expenditure Tax in India* (1992), Readings *in Islamic Fiscal Policy* (1996), *Islamic Public Economics* (2001), *Islamic Public Finance and Policy* (2004), *On Islamic Taxation,* and *Economics of Taxation* (2010). He has also published more than 50 research papers some of which have appeared in *Indian Journal of Economics, Finance India, Pakistan Development Review, Islamia University Bahawalpur Journal of Economics* and *King Abdul Aziz University Journal of Islamic Economics.*

Contents

Preface

In this work, an attempt is made to study the economic ideas of Caliph Ali (600-661 C.E.). In the writings on Islamic economic thought, not much literature is available that throws light on the economic thought of Ali, before and after he became the Caliph.

The conventional history of advancement of knowledge acknowledges the contribution of Greek and Roman scholars until around 300 C.E. and then picks up the trail again in 1500 C.E., i.e. the beginning of the Renaissance. A period of 1200 years, between 300 C.E. and 1500 C.E. is left out. Morotowitz describes this phenomenon as 'history's black hole' and Schumpeter talks about a 'great gap'. They maintain and claim that the Renaissance somehow arose like a "phoenix" from the "ashes" which had been smouldering for a millennium since the classical age of Greece and Rome.

The above-mentioned claim of Morotowitz and Schumpeter is totally unfounded. They were not aware of the Muslim contribution, starting from early 7th century. It is in order to say that, alone in the area of public finances, Muslim scholars produced more than a dozen works during the period which they refer to as 'history's black hole' and 'great gap'.

In popular works on the economic thought, there is no mention of social, political and economic thought of the Muslims scholars. Ali and several other great thinkers are ignored. In this way, there is a great gap in the literature and not in the history. The present work intends to fill this gap to some extent.

A systematic study of the economic ideas of Ali makes it clear that he was a distinct precursor to several economic values, which even today continue to dominate the mainstream economic thinking worldwide. He excelled in both letter and spirit, whenever a new economic problem or issue came before him. The justification, which Ali provided on several economic issues, was amazingly incredible and never heard before.

The present work is spread over eight chapters. Chapter 1 is introductory. Chapter 2 deals with the early developments after the demise of the Prophet; the conduct of Ali after the Prophet; and the role of Ali as an advisor and the selection of Ali as the Caliph. Chapter 3 sheds light on the values which Ali upheld and for which he sacrificed his life. Economic policy earlier to Ali is discussed in Chapter 4. It also deals with the economic vision of Ali. Post-Caliphate economic policy of Ali with special reference to the mobilization and distribution of resources is examined in Chapter 5. It is followed by Chapter 6 wherein there is a discussion on Ali's economic and social concerns. Chapter 7 deals with Ali's views on the need for a good government and its subsequent benefits. The concluding Chapter 8 summarizes the essence of Alinomics.

I place on record my deep sense of gratitude to Islamic scholars Mr. M.G. Mahaldar, and Janab Shabir Ahmad Khan, and my son Dr. S.M. Meraj Hussaini for providing useful and critical comments on an earlier draft of this work. Their comments and suggestions helped me to improve the contents of this work, where necessary.

I am equally grateful to New Century Publications, New Delhi, for taking keen interest in the publication of this work. Nevertheless, I am alone responsible for errors, if any.

Bijapur **Sayed Afzal Peerzade**

1

Introduction

Alinomics

Alinomics is a term, which is coined here to mean a systematic study of economic ideas of Ali (600-661 C.E.) who is, according to the Sunni doctrine, a pious and austere man, a close companion of the Prophet and the fourth righteous caliph. The Shias all over the world hold him as the first *imam* in a chain of twelve *aaimah* (sngl. *imam*). To an equally large number of Muslims across the world, he is a peerless mystic master who publicly and privately practiced highest level of abstinence and detachment from material comforts. He is one of the earliest spiritual masters and often regarded as the first link to the Prophet in Sufi *salasil* (chains/orders).

A systematically dispassionate study of the economic ideas of Ali makes it clear that he was a distinct precursor to several economic values, which even today continue to dominate the mainstream economic thinking worldwide. He excelled in both letter and spirit, whenever a new economic problem or issue came before him. The justification, which Ali provided on several economic issues, was amazingly incredible and never heard before.

In the history of Islam, the role of Ali is multifarious. He is one of the persons who put faith in the Prophet immediately after the declaration of the prophet-hood (610 C.E.). He proved a truthful companion of the Prophet (570-632 C.E.) who shared with him the moments of joy, grief and sufferings. Historians have applauded his knowledge of Islamic doctrines and law, his love for Islam and the Prophet and his heroic role in the early battles of Islam.

Ali's conscientious statesmanship and principled political stand are universally acknowledged. The impact of Ali's personal charm, noble qualities, magnetism of character and spell of ideas was so deep, intense and long lasting that its hangover continues even today. His commitment to the cause of socio-economic equality remains undisputed.

Objectives

Not much is written on various aspects of Ali's accomplishments. So also, not much literature is available to highlight the sincere cooperation, which Ali extended to his predecessors as well as the critical or rather highly complex situation prevailing during his caliphate (656-661 C.E.). He had to face precarious state of affairs. Similarly not much light is shed on the political and administrative policies he pursued and the moral and Islamic values he upheld even in the most trying circumstances. His vision of caliphate and mission of governance are also not studied thoroughly. It is in this context that the present work has following principal objectives, although these are limited in their own way:

1. To introduce economic policy in Islam in general and economic ideas of Ali in particular to the non-Muslim readers of economic thought in Islam.
2. To develop a personal profile of Ali.
3. To study economic thought and vision of Ali.
4. To study economic policy which Ali pursued during his period of caliphate.

Scant Attention

In recent years, researchers have admitted that that there are "innumerable guides of humanity, flag bearers of reform, builders of nations and countries and teachers of wisdom and learning whose real accomplishments have remained unknown to the world for hundreds of years. One of these victimized personalities whose real worth was never appreciated was Ali bin Abu Talib. The demands of the age in which he lived and difficulties which he faced were never dispassionately analyzed". [1]

Similarly, Ali's economic ideas have received insufficient attention. Till this day, we have two exhaustive surveys of works on Islamic economics.

One is done by Siddiqui [2] and another one by Sabry Shaban of Astana-e-Quds Razvi. [3] It appears from the surveys that as far as topical emphases are concerned, the following areas are hugely covered by the researchers: Islamic economic system, Islamic critique of Contemporary Economic theories, economic philosophy of Islam, history of Islamic economic thought, and Economic Analysis in Islamic Framework. The areas, which have recorded maximum publications, are: interest free banking, insurance and investment, social security, Islamic public finance especially *zakah,* role of the state and land ownership. As far as writings on Islamic economic thought are concerned, the highest numbers of publications are on Ibn Khaldun, Ibn Taimiyyah and Abu Yusuf.

Details of Different Works Surveyed by Siddiqui

1.	Economic Philosophy of Islam	80 entries
2.	Economic System of Islam	417 entries
3.	Economic Critique of Islam	110 entries
4.	Economic Analysis in Islamic Framework	37 entries
5.	History of Economic Thought	43 entries
•	Ibn Khaldun	13 entries
•	Ibn Taimiyah	03 entries
•	Abu Yusuf	05 entries
•	Yahyah ibn Adam	03 entries
•	Abu Jafar Dimishqi	02 entries
•	Nasir al Din Tusi	02 entries

In the same volume, there is survey of Turkish works wherein we find 220 entries on the topics mentioned above. [4] In the survey conducted by Sabry Shaban the entries are as shown in the table below:

Details of Different Works Surveyed by Sabry Shaban

1.	Economic view of Islam	123 entries
2.	Critique of Contemporary Economic Theories and Systems from Islamic Perspective	078 entries
3.	Islamic Economics: Theory and System	1,417 entries
4.	Toward Developing Islamic Economic Science	137 entries
5.	Economics of Muslim countries and fields of their Cooperation:	178 entries
6.	Islamic Economics Practices	126 entries
7.	Islamic Economic History	666 entries
8.	Bibliographies, Encyclopaedias, etc.	074 entries
9.	Miscellaneous	094 entries

In all, Sabry Shaban has covered 2,467 titles of different authors and reports, etc., prepared by different institutions/banks/organizations. However, a serious drawback of this survey is that the work/s by the same author/s appear/s in different categories and hence there is a repetition. Nevertheless, when repetition is avoided, the number is still large. The object of our study has hardly received adequate attention.

This work, to a little extent, intends to fill this gap by covering a few important aspects of Ali's economic thought and policy. There is no major work devoted exclusively to the study of economic ideas of Ali in a systematic and methodological way. Several passing references are made to his ideas, sayings and actions but these remain scattered. Ali's moral, spiritual and juristic contributions have overshadowed his economic ideas, principles and administration. Several authors who have written exhaustively on life, times and works of Ali, have not paid adequate attention to his economics ideas. Since Ali's economic ideas were not properly identified, the question of their analytical study did not arise.

Research Questions

The present work on the economic ideas of Ali broadly

addresses the following research questions:

1. What was Ali's economic vision and mission?
2. What economic policy Ali followed when the situation at the time of his caliphate was highly perplexing?
3. How unique are Ali's economic ideas?

Major Sources

Ever since the early years of Islam, sayings, sermons and letters of Ali especially his unparalleled sermons, have attracted the attention of the literati as well as the common people. Those familiar with the intricate beauties of the Arabic language, had collected or compiled these works for posterity. Abu al-Hasan Mas'udi (d. 346 A.H.), the historian par excellence, is of the opinion that people had memorized hundreds of his sermons and sayings. In the collections of traditions of the Prophet, several references are available to *Musnad Ali ibn Abi Talib.* [5] Much before Sayyid Razi [6] (359-404 A.H) compiled his magnum opus *Nahjul Balagha*, several scholars had collected, in book-form, the sayings, sermons and judgments of Ali.

In *Kanzul-Ummal* also we find several references to the sayings, sermons and actions of Ali. This compilation of the traditions is spread over spread over 16 volumes and contains 46,624 narrations. The author of this colossal work is Alauddin Ali Muttaqi bin Hussamuddin Burhanpuri (India). In religious circles, he is popularly known as al-Muttaqi al-Hindi (975/1567). It is claimed about this compilation that its study is equivalent to a study of seventy different compilations of the traditions. [7]

Another major source is Abu Ubaid's (d.224 A.H.) classical work *Kitab al-Amwaal*. [8]. Among the early known works dealing with Islamic public finance, Abu Ubaid's book occupies chronologically the third position after *Kitab al-Kharaj* of Qadi Abu Yusuf (d. 182 A.H.) and *Kitab al Kharaj* of Yahya ibn Adam (d.203 A.H.). [9] It is a highly systematic work arranged on the lines as we expect from any modern text on public finance. It is spread over two sections, ninety-one chapters and contains 1997 narrations. At several places, where several traditions concerning one issue are quoted, Abu Ubaid has taken his own stand and has tried to justify the same. Herein, next only to the Prophet and Umar, Ali is quoted profusely.

Our major source, however, is *Nahjul Balagha (Peak of Eloquence).* The topics or subjects of *Nahjul Balagha* are broad and varied. A few of which are enumerated as follows: theology and the supernatural; manners and worship, government and justice, world and worldliness, epic and bravery, poetical saga and mysteries, supplications, criticism of people's behaviour, social principles, Islam and Qur'an, ethics and self-reform, personalities, leadership and leaders, life of Ali, wars during his caliphate, state policy, social affairs, personal affairs, maxims and advices, fundamentals of religion and practical laws, society, politics and economy, fear and hope, repentance, forgiveness of sins, enjoining of good and forbidding of evil, *jihad,* battle techniques and martyrdom, ruler and his qualities, etc. The compilation consists of 238 *khutab (*orations); 78 *rasa'il* (epistles); 473 *hikam* (maxims); and 9 *gharib* (sayings including rare words). In modern times, it is translated into more than thirty languages. It is also noted that the actual number of sermons far exceed those compiled in *Nahjul Balagha.*

So far, Muslim scholars have made a few attempts to classify the subject matter of the book. [10] Alone the *Ma'rifat nizam al-hukumah wa al-mujtama* part is divided into twenty-three *fusul* (chapters):

1. The most fundamental objectives and duties of Islamic government.
2. The characteristics of rulers.
3. The duties of rulers toward people.
4. Ministers and advisers.
5. People's rights: social classes and their mutual dependence; responsibilities of the army; and

functions of rulers in fulfilling people's rights.
6. The Islamic army and choice of commanders.
7. The mutual rights of people and rulers.
8. Resolution of differences.
9. Courts of justice and *qadis.*
10. Officials and functionaries of government, their mode of selection; the ruler's duty toward them.
11. Information and intelligence of the State, and military intelligence.
12. Taxes, public treasury and taxpayers: means of levying taxes; protection and guarding of public treasury; heads of expenditure of public funds; equitable distribution of and problems of misappropriation of *bayt al-maal.*
13. Secretaries and record-keepers of official matters (ministers and high officials).
14. Businessmen and industrialists administration of economic affairs, and government's supervision of economic matters of the State.
15. The oppressed and the deprived sections of society, and ruler's duties toward them.
16. Governors' direct contact with people for listening to their grievances, and people's right to have access to rulers.
17. Governors' personal responsibility in certain matters.
18. Direct supervision by governors and government authorities of current affairs of the state.
19. Ruler, his family and relatives.
20. Duty of governors' *vis-à-vis* charges levelled against them.
21. Pacts and peace treaties with other States.
22. Guidelines for performance of governors' individual and social functions.
23. Seeking God's help for being just.

It is a matter of concern that Syed al-Razi, the compiler of *Nahjul Balagha*, has not paid due attention to support many of the sermons, letters and sayings with *asnad* (the chain of narrators). As a result, *Nahjul Balagha* comes down to us in the form of a *hadith mursal.* [11]. However, for cross checking, we have access to many early sources of these traditions to prove their authenticity through the chain of reliable narrators, and most probably, al-Razi did not pay attention to furnish their *asnad* due to their availability in other sources.

Islamic Economic System

The study of Islamic economic system did not receive its due attention in the past for the reason that the discussion on economic and financial issues was more juristic than economic in nature. Inadequate attention may be also attributed to a system of education inherited from the imperial powers who successfully segregated Islamic education from modern education. On one hand, primary sources remained in Arabic on the other English was made the language of teaching, research and communication. The professionally trained economists had either no or limited access to the primary sources. This inhibited professional economists from making any significant contribution to this subject. Works in English by professional economists on this subject appeared in the late forties of previous century only but these writers had to rely on secondary sources as far as Islamic economic doctrines were concerned.

Islamic economics is based on the *shariah,* which Muslims believe is sacred and inviolable. This is, of course, due to their profound belief in Islam as a divine religion transmitted by the last Prophet, and to their belief that Islam does not limit itself to a set of prayers and worship only but is rather a way of life, a political, social and economic ordering of the Islamic community.

Islam appeared fifteen centuries ago in a primitive period, an era of slavery and underdevelopment as far as economics is concerned. It is normally held that the doctrines of economics reflect the period of their origin. However, Islamic doctrines transcend time and space mainly on account of their divine character. Islam stood, from the very beginning, for true equality and a share of poor in the riches of wealthy. It developed an economic balance amongst the conflicting as well as competing interests of society and confirmed the principle of dual ownership (i.e. private and public). It favoured 'state-intervention' in the economy wherever and whenever required.

The Essence of Islamic Economics

In economic domain, two opposing trends are discernable in the world, the capitalist and the socialist. The capitalist system stands free enterprise and private ownership of means of production. It embodies in itself the ideas of classical and neo-classical economists who believed in the efficiency of market forces, minimal role of the government and a policy of laissez faire. Adam Smith, the father of Economics, believed in the powers of 'invisible hand'. This 'invisible hand', in 19th century, became an iconic symbol.

However, certain developments in early 20th century paralyzed 'invisible hand'. The most important of all was the Great Depression of 1930s. The 'invisible hand' miserably failed to control markets in avoiding cyclical fluctuations. It also failed to check income, consumption and wealth inequalities. The other development namely the Russian Revolution of 1917 made the followers of classical ideas more sceptical than before. The publication John Maynard Keynes's epoch making work *The General Theory* favoured state intervention. However, capitalism could survive and still survives because its overall approach was flexible enough to accommodate human instincts of holding private property and wealth.

The Marxian ideology heralded on the economic scene with a big bang. It represented an alternative economic and political thought as developed by Karl Marx. It enjoyed a great success for at least seven decades after which cracks developed in the system. The communist alternative collapsed under the weight of its own ideology and miserably failed to accommodate and honour 'natural human instinct', which serves the purpose of cog in the super wheel of economic machinery.

Currently, the above-mentioned dominant economic philosophies do not survive in their pristine form. What we find today in practice is a hybrid system of mixed economy wherein we find a convergence of capitalist and communist ideas in varying forms. This is not to mean that the convergence has met the needs of our times. We continue to come across complaints of various types. Crises, one after another and of one type or the other, are haunting world economy, which because of revolutions in telecommunications and transportation, has turned into a global village economy.

In the context of these developments, let us proceed to examine the Islamic economic approach. An essential feature of Islamic economics is that each and every economic issue is understood and approached with a minimum critical reference to the *shariah.* The *shariah* reminds us that: [12]

1. Almighty Allah knows as to what we have done, what we are doing at present and what we plan to do in the future.
2. All our actions, dealings and transactions are for the sake of Allah.
3. We are held responsible for our actions in our various capacities such as consumers, traders, producers, etc., and we are rewarded or punished accordingly.
4. Our stay in this world is but a brief stopover and we have to prepare ourselves for a journey hereafter.
5. The motives governing our actions should not harm the interest of others.
6. We should be very careful regarding what is proper and improper; legal and illegal; good and bad and moral and immoral.
7. We should use our energy for productive purposes and we should not damage and obstruct others' constructive activities.

8. We should suggest only those solutions to others, which benefit them.

The discipline of Islamic economics, accords due importance to an individual. It is because of the fact that, from amongst other economic agents, he is dynamic, self-motivated and energetic. He is the ruler and ruled. He frames laws, follows them and more often than not breaks them. On one hand, he ensures higher supplies through efficient management of resources, on the other creates artificial scarcity, and engages himself in black marketing and profiteering. His behaviour, characterized by different contrasts, greatly affects the growth path of communities and nations. It is in this backdrop that he is asked to strictly follow the footsteps of the Prophet.

The Quranic code of conduct in its entirety is reflected in the life of the Prophet. The economic message delivered by the Prophet is revolutionary in character and yet simple and objective in its disposition. Purely from economic viewpoint, three distinguishing features of the life of the Prophet can be identified as under:

1. Austerity in personal life.
2. Rigor in public life.
3. Concern for poor and deserving.

The essence of ethical and moral injunctions deriving their support from the life of the Prophet is that one should lead a simple life and exercise austerity. Today, it seems that austerity is the only way out from the economic crises. Modern governments and rulers should take a leaf from the life of the Prophet as to how he managed the affairs of the then rapidly expanding Islamic state. The righteous caliphs, who followed the Prophetic code of conduct, both at personal and public levels, took Islamic state from strength to strength. It is also recalled here that the disintegration of mighty Muslim states in the past was due to a lavish consumption expenditure of their rulers and a total disregard to the Islamic code of conduct.

With the passage of time, Muslims have realized that their

salvation is in going back to the fundamentals of Islam. Neither capitalism nor socialism is capable of solving their economic problems for the reason that there arises a clash of values and not of civilizations. Capitalism believes that an enlightened self-interest will eventually work to the benefit of all.

The Marxists hold that the production and means of production must be controlled by the state to ensure a just and equal share of all benefits of human endeavour. The advocates of capitalism claim that the institutions of private enterprise and private property enable an economy first to achieve and then to sustain high growth rates. These in turn generate employment opportunities and minimize the difference between rich and poor. The Marxists, on the other, do not at all believe in classes and therefore the question of rich and poor does not fit into their scheme of things.

We should not discard outright the ideals of capitalism and socialism. The two have done wonders. Capitalist states have achieved tremendous economic power, which contributed to their political and military might. The economic power benefited and in turn was benefited by the scientific advances, in addition to social and political enlightenment. Similarly, the socialist states did create extraordinary infrastructure and, largely, they succeeded in protecting their people from the vagaries of market mechanism such as unemployment, inequalities, poverty and price rise.

It is a universal fact that only that system will stand to the test of time, which is natural. Even though centuries ago the true Islamic state ceased to exist, the message of Islam remains fresh even today. It appeals to everyone crossing the barriers of time and regions. An essential feature of a natural system is that it avoids anything that is extreme. In fact, extremism of any type has no place in Islam.

The Islamic economic system sprouted from divine revelation, it being a light that descended upon the Prophet. As and when human prudence fails, the foresight of the Prophet comes to its rescue. The Islamic economic system, therefore, does not set classes against one another but asks different stakeholders to respect the excellence and rights of others. It prohibits one class from injuring economic interests of another class. It does not approve the domination of one class over the other. Each class is asked to behave well within the limits of *shariah*.

We can easily understand the essence of Islamic economic system in the context of private property rights. The property rights are governed by four basic principles. The first principle asserts that the Almighty is the Absolute and Ultimate Owner of property. The second principle maintains that the Almighty has granted possession and control over property to men as His trustees. The third principle argues that the property is only a means of achieving higher objectives and not an end in itself. On the Day of Reckoning, men are taken to task regarding the exercise of property rights. The fourth principle, called as the principle of sharing of ownership, is derived from the first two. This establishes the right of society in general and that of poor in particular in the riches of wealthy. Islam has institutionalized the process of welfare promotion much before the modern welfare economists and the states could think of 'the compensation principle'. [13]

Even though, the Islamic economic system shares certain values with both capitalism and socialism, yet it has a specific orientation and a distinctive policy. Moreover, even if the latter resembles other economic policies in various aspects it remains, nevertheless, unique since it is:

1. A static and dynamic policy at the same time. It is static in principles and foundations. It is also a dynamic policy because its basic tenets are flexible enough to accommodate different methods of application.
2. A policy that serves both the personal and common interests. It ignores neither the interest of the community nor that of an individual. The Islamic economic policy is rather, from the start, concerned with both the interests and

tries to maintain a balance.

3. If this harmony or equilibrium were not possible in the extraordinary circumstances then the common interest would prevail over individual interest.
4. A policy that serves material welfare as well as spiritual needs. It considers individual economic activity pious and noble as long as it is planned and oriented for the cause of the Almighty and for the service of His creatures.

In Islam, there is no conflict of interest between matter and soul; this worldly and otherworldly affairs; physical and metaphysical values. This is for the reason that there is no separation between economy and religion and between mosque and the state. There is rather a strong integration amongst them, a fact that guarantees success in this world and in the Hereafter. Since Islam holds man as the "viceroy of Allah on His earth", his intent of economic actions will be to make the world a better living place for the creature of Allah.

The Nature and Scope of Economic Policy in Islam

Based on the above discussion, we may summarise that the economic policy in Islam presents three major elements.

1. It accommodates what is stable and what is not. This is the characteristic of the doctrine and the system.
2. It accommodates public and private interests. This is the harmonization of conflicting interests.
3. It accommodates material interests and spiritual needs. This is the harmonization of 'this world' and 'other world' interests.

From the very beginning the economic system in Islam is bound to *shariah* based economic principles. Nevertheless, it does leave the door open for experimentation so that each Muslim nation can choose what goes best with its interests. In this sense, a Muslim nation can choose the system advocating public interest while another can opt for the opposite system. Economy in either case will remain Muslim as long as it abides by the idea of public and private dichotomy, since the difference between the two is a difference in their application depending on the time and the place.

The Islamic economic system during the period of righteous caliphs was exemplary in its application of Islamic principles in the context of the then socio-economic and political conditions. Now that the economic and social lives of people have become more complicated, Muslim nations may not experience difficulties in designing their economic approach in the context of above mentioned principles.

The Spiritual Content in Islamic Economics

Even though Islam acknowledges the material element and material profit in economic activities, it does not neglect, however, the spiritual instinct in men and women. In his commercial transaction, a man is required to seek the Lord in order to gain His grace. Islam holds every material activity practiced by Muslims as a spiritual act as long as it remains lawful and geared towards Allah, the Almighty. It is simply not true that there is a conflict between religion and worldly life, or that there is one domain for activities in this life and another for those in the Hereafter. Islam provides a healthy balance between affairs of the world *(dunya)* and those of religion *(din)*.

The choice between the world and religion is not both this or that but both this and that. Islam recognizes this metaphysical division between the material and the spiritual needs only on the basis of lawfulness embodied in Allah's pleasure. The Prophet told to his companions that even the mundane affairs are considered as worship of Allah. If a person is out in search of his child's food then he is acting in the Way of the Lord. If he is out to seek food for his elderly parents, then he is acting in the Way of the Lord. If he is out to find his own food then he is acting in the Way of the Lord. However, if he is out seeking glory (for himself), then he is acting for Satan's sake.

Moreover, the true sign of faith in Islam is doing good

deeds and producing what is useful to the society. Allah, the Almighty, says in this respect "And say: "Work (righteousness): soon will God observe your work, and His Apostle, and the believers: Soon will ye be brought back to the Knower of what is hidden and what is open: Then will He show you the truth of all that ye did" (9:105).

The Prophet likewise suggests that the most effective way to reach the Lord and gain His Grace is to love and help His people. The Prophet remarked that Allah loves more those who are most useful to others. Allah, the Almighty, says during the Day of Judgment: 'O son of Adam, I fell ill but you did not visit Me. He will say O Lord, how could I visit You when You are the Lord of the Worlds? He will say: Did you not know that My servant had fallen ill and you did not visit him? Did you not know that had you visited him you would have found Me with him, O son of Adam, I asked you for food, but you did not feed Me. He will say: O Lord, how could I feed You when You are the Lord of the Worlds? He will say: Did you not know that my servant asked you for food and you did not feed him? Did you not know that had you fed him you would surely have found your reward with Me? O son of Adam, I asked you for water and you gave Me no drink, He will say: O Lord, how could I give You water to drink when You are the Lord of the worlds? He will say My servant asked you to give him to drink and you did not give him water to drink. Did you not know that had you given him water to drink, you would have found your reward with Me? [14]

Control in Islamic Economics

In addition to the formal regulatory measures, the economic activities in Islam are controlled by a firm faith in Allah and in the Day of Judgment. This ensures a sound social and economic behaviour. A sound behaviour ensures economic prosperity in the sense that the competitive agents do not compete just for their own self-interest. One competing agent will not create problems for others and vice versa. The faith will help them to rise above the limited and restrictive self-interest. They are serving not to others to serve themselves, but are serving to serve the cause of Almighty. Indeed the believer feels that if he can avoid control of the law, he certainly cannot escape from the grip of Allah, "the All Knower All Wise". It appears in one of the traditions of the Prophet that we should worship Allah as if we see Him, but if we cannot see Him, He surely sees us all. The Prophet has also declared that at the moment of committing crime, an adulterous or a thief is not a believer.

We conclude from the preceding discussion that Islam creates a sense of religious restraint in economic activities. The restraint is a feeling of the Muslim that he is under the Lord's control in every transaction that he carries out, and that he will be held accountable. The system of economics in Islam, hence, encourages a religious control. A practicing Muslim, out of his deep faith, respects Islamic laws voluntarily. Since, there is no separation between *din* and *dunya*, a believer abides by the rules, which are applicable to both, the worldly and otherworldly affairs.

Material interest is an aim in itself in all positivist systems. This is true whether the aim is to ensure the maximum profit as in capitalism or sufficiency and material prosperity as in socialism. There is no doubt that the materialist economic systems, both capitalist and socialist, have realized various gains and higher levels of prosperity. These, however, are bound to disappear due to a hysterical conflict that ravages the essence of these systems as long as material profit and self-interest dominate the scene. The recurrence of economic crises in United States is before us. Not much time has passed since the disintegration of once mighty USSR.

Even though material interest is also an aim in Islamic economics, it is not an end in itself. Rather, it is a means to guarantee the success and happiness at the personal and collective levels. Islam views this life as a preparatory step to the Hereafter. Moreover, if the Muslim is required to make money and makes it grow, he does not do so for money's sake. He considers it as an effective means of serving humanity. The possession of wealth is appreciated when it facilitates worship of Allah more meaningfully.

This is why the Prophet has said that 'great is the money when it helps a man worship Allah'. Moreover, the Almighty says: "Do ye not see that God has subjected to your (use) all things in the heavens and on earth, and has made His bounties flow to you in exceeding measure (both) seen and unseen? Yet there are among men those who dispute about God."(31:20). The Lord also said: "It is He who hadth made your (His) agents, inheritors of the earth; He hath raised you in ranks, some above others; that He may try you in the gifts He hath given you; for thy Lord is quick in punishment; yet He is indeed oft-forgiving, Most Merciful" (6:165). We can, thus argue, here that there is a room in Islam for the "desirability of what is material". The Almighty says in this respect "And when the Prayer is finished, then may ye disperse through the land, and seek of the bounty of God; and celebrate the praises of God often (and without stint) that ye may proper" (62:10). In addition: "It is We Who have placed you with authority on earth, and provided You therein with means for the fulfilment of your life; small are the thanks that ye give" (7:10).

Summing Up

We draw the following three major conclusions from the analysis so far:

1. Economic policy in Islam is not restricted to the promotion of material benefits only. It accommodates them with the spiritual needs and aspirations of people. This policy is based on the belief in Allah, the Almighty, and on one's own responsibility toward Him. This is what gives Islamic economics its characteristic of belief and spirituality purported by the need to be in the presence of Allah in all commercial transactions.
2. Islam introduces an element of self-control. The control

over economic activities in Islam is dual in its nature, in the sense that it is not based on outwardly laws only, but on the belief in Allah that He is watching us and to Whom we are all accountable.

3. The material progress is not sought for its own sake, but for the prosperity of mankind. The aim of economic policy is the realization of harmony between different peoples and nations, and not the encouragement of conflict and killing.

End Notes

1. Nadwi, Sayed Abul Hasan Ali, *Al-Murtuza*, Academy of Islamic Research and Publications, Lucknow, 3rd Edition, 1991. The present author has followed its English translation entitled *The Life of Caliph Ali.* It was rendered into English by S. Mohiuddin Ahmed and published by Academy of Islamic Research and Publications, Lucknow, 1991, p. 2.
2. Siddiqui, Muhammad Nejatullah, "Muslims Economics Thinking: A Survey of Contemporary Literature" in Khursheed Ahmad (ed.) *First International Conference on Islamic Economics: Selected Papers*, Amar Prakashan, Delhi, 1984.
3. Shaban, Sabry S., *A Classified Bibliography on Islamic Economics,* Part I-III, Islamic Research Foundation of Astan-e-Quds Razvi, Islamic Economics Department, Mashad, Iran, 1989.
4. Zaim, Sasahuddin, "Contemporary Turkish Literature on Islamic Economics", in Khursheed Ahmad (ed.), *First International Conference on Islamic Economics: Selected Papers*, Amar Prakashan, Delhi, 1984.
5. A great scholar from Indian sub-continent, Shah Waliullah Muhadith Dehlvi, in his magnum opus *Izalatul Khulfa* (Urdu Edition), in two volumes, Maktab-e-Hafizi, Deoband, undated, has referred to *Musnad Ali ibn Abu Talib* pp.154-164.
6. Abul Hussan Syed Mohammed Razi was born in Baghdad in 359 A.H. in a highly respected family which was held in great regards by Abbasid caliphs. His father Abu Ahmed Syed Hussain was appointed five times as Naqueeb or chief of the members of the family of Ali. At the age of 21 years, he was elected in the place of his father as Naqueeb. He died (404 A.H.) at the young age of forty-four years. In addition to the

compilation of *Nahjul Balagha* he has left behind commentaries on Quran and traditions of the Prophet. In all, he has penned forty books.

7. The present author has followed Urdu translation of *Kanz al-ummal* published by Idarah-e-Isha'at-e-Islam, Deoband, India, 2010.
8. Abu Ubaid Al Qasim bin Sallam, *Kitab al Amwal,* Urdu Edition, Idarah-e-Tahqiqat-e-Islami, Islamabad, Pakistan, 1986.
9. The other important works are those of Abu'l Faraj Qudamah ibn Jafar al-Khatib (d. 320 A.H.) *Kitab al Kharaj*; Abu Jafar Ahmad ibn Nasr al-Daudi (d. 402 A.H.)'s *Kitab al Amwal* and Abu'l Faraj Abd al Rahman ibn Rajab al-Hanbali (d.795 A.H.)'s *Kitab al-Kharaj.*
10. Sayyid Razi was able to collect only a part of the sermons, letters and maxims of Ali. A Lebanese scholar Sayyid Sadiq Musavi has collected the sermons, letters and maxims of Ali from the libraries across the world. It took 18 years of incessant work. For this purpose he visited more than 150 libraries in India, Iran, Iraq, Lebanon, Syria, Egypt, Yemen, Tunisia, Morocco, UK, France, USA, Spain and Canada and referred more than seventy thousand books. These are compiled in eight volumes in Arabic and entitled as "*Tamam Nahjul Balagha*" *[The Complete Nahjul Balagha]* which contains 800 subjects.
11. If the narrator between the successor and the Prophet is omitted from a given *isnād*, the hadith is *mursal.*
12. Peerzade, Sayed Afzal, *On Taxation in Islam,* Idarah-i- Adbiyat-e-Dilli, Delhi, 2009, p. 10.
13. Peerzade, Sayed Afzal, "Quranic Perspective of Compensation Principle", *Proceedings of Seminar on Economic Problems and The Teachings of Quran"*, Idarah Uloom al-Quran, Shibli Bagh, Aligarh, 2010, pp. 178-186.
14. For a detailed account of Quranic verses and traditions of the Prophet pertaining to economic issues one may refer to Monzar Kahf's *Al-nusus,* King Abdul Aziz University, Jeddah, 1990.

2

From Companionship to the Caliphate

The Early Developments

The Prophet of Islam passed away, at the age of sixty-three years, on 8th of June, 632 C.E. at Madinah leaving his mission totally accomplished. [1] The Prophet left behind no son, nor any specific written will. [2] However, all the companions agreed upon the necessity of electing one amongst them as the leader. The nearest relatives of the Prophet were Abu Bakr, his father in law and two years younger than the Prophet; Umar, the father in law and eighteen years younger; Usman, his son in law, five years younger and Ali, his son in law, about thirty years younger. This difference in the age became decisive in the choice of caliph. [3] "In the leadership of the tribe, there was never acknowledged among the Bedouin tribes a fixed order of hereditary succession. It was regarded as something extraordinary if the leadership of a tribe continued in one and the same family for four generations". [4]

At the time of passing away of the Prophet, the Arabs were trembling with energy and faith, ready to explode on the world. Within decades, they had arrived at Spain in the West and Sind in the East. The world had not seen anything like that before. The Roman conquest had been slow and steady. Alexander, the Great, was like a meteor and immediately after he died his empire fell apart. The Muslims brought with them a fresh civilization, a new way of looking at living the life; they had come to stay and influence others.

All over the world Muslims regard the period of Muhammad and the first generation of companions as normative for a variety of reasons. "First, God sent down His final and complete revelation, the Quran, and the last of His prophets, Muhammad. Second, the Islamic community-state was created, bonded by a common religious identity and purpose. Third, the sources of Islamic law, the Quran and the example of the Prophet, originated at this time. Fourth, this period of early companions served as the reference point for all Islamic revival and reform movements, both traditionalist and modernist. Fifth, the success and power that resulted from the near-miraculous victories and geographic expansion of Islam constitute, in the eyes of believers, historical validation of the message of Islam". [5]

The unexpected demise of the Prophet came as a rude shock to his followers. Suddenly, they were at loss to decide about the future course of action. The enemies of Islam and newly born Islamic state, both within and without, were carefully watching all these developments. They were waiting for an appropriate time to strike a lethal blow. They, however, could not succeed mainly because of two reasons. First, the Prophet had laid a very sound political and administrative foundation of the society and state. Secondly, the men very close to the Prophet were persons of highest sincerity and integrity. These two factors, immediately after the Prophet, prevented the early Islamic state from a possible disintegration.

Deep Foundations

We attempt here to identify a few salient principles on which the Prophet and his immediate caliphs laid the political and administrative foundation of the early Islamic state:

1. The head of the state should not lead a life of luxury, extravagance and ostentation.
2. Simplicity, both inward and outward, should be an essential feature of public conduct.
3. The personal conduct of the head of the state should be above any doubt.
4. Governance is a trust of Almighty Allah. It should not be regarded as a personal or private affair to be managed by a few.
5. Caliphate should be considered as a public institution wherein everyone should have his or her say.

6. All efforts should be made to make the government people-based. Public consultation should be made a regular feature of the governance.
7. Delivery of justice should be quick, effective and almost costless. Equality before the law should be an openly declared principle.
8. Institutional arrangements should be made to collect and distribute levies.
9. Earmarked spending should be practiced.
10. Control of evil and perfidious activities should be made a public function of the government and public power should be used as a means of reform.

The Prophet and his immediate caliphs succeeded in laying a sound political foundation of the newly established Islamic state. Judged from any standard, their conduct, both at the public and personal levels, was exemplary. None, even their worst opponents, ever had an iota of doubt about their personal sincerity and integrity. Their conduct left a deep and profound impact upon the public at large. It provided, without doubt, necessary political authority to run the affairs of the state in general and to raise the required revenue in particular. The morality and piety of the Prophet and his rightly guided caliphs, in fact, greatly strengthened the political foundation. It is not wrong here to emphasize that their moral force was a source of their political authority. In the then Islamic state, power originated from the morality, neither from the "barrel of a gun" nor from the "seat of authority".

Prerequisites of a Caliph

Now, it is necessary to know the requirements, which the then Islamic state demanded from the caliph. [6]

1. He must have enjoyed full confidence of the Prophet ever since his acceptance of Islam;
2. The Prophet must have avouched his sincerity, entrusted to him the responsibility of acting on his behalf, particularly in matters relating to religion, and taken him in confidence

in delicate affairs and on perilous occasions.

3. He should be a man of indomitable courage and conviction..
4. He should have a deep comprehension of religious truth and imbibed its spirit to the extent that he was never unmindful of the example set by the Prophet.
5. Pristine purity and integrity of faith should have been a thing more cherished and precious to him than the honour of his own person or family.
6. He should have always been prepared to make the greatest sacrifice for the faith, unshaken by any fear or favour.
7. He should have made it the aim and purpose of his life to follow the teachings of the Prophet without deflecting a hair's breadth from them.
8. He should have been unmindful of riches, fame, and personal conveniences.
9. His character should have been so spotless that he never ever conceived of taking any personal advantage of his position as a ruler or allowed his family members to derive the slightest benefit from his status, marking a complete break from the traditions of royalty in the neighbouring countries.

Al-Ghazali, in the following narration, makes clear the public perception of the caliphate and caliph. A learned man once told Abbasid Caliph Harun' ur Rashid [7] to be careful that he was sitting where Abu Bakr once sat and was truthful; where Umar once sat and differentiated between right and wrong; where Usman once sat and was modest and bountiful and where Ali once sat and was erudite and just. Al-Ghazali showcases the Prophet who himself fed his cattle, tied his camel, swept his house, milked his goad, sewed his shoes, patched his clothes, took meals with his servant, ground his own corn in time of need and did his own marketing. [8]

Ali after the Prophet

Immediately after the passing away of the Prophet, Abu

Bakr, his long-time companion, was chosen to lead the Muslims. When the tension between *muhajirun* and *ansar* over the choice of a caliph started developing, Umar immediately sensed its adverse repercussions. He came forward to swear allegiance to Abu Bakr. This step of Umar had salutary impact because Umar's personality was indeed towering. He commanded respect from all quarters and was feared by many. Any inaction by this responsible and lifelong companion of the Prophet would have caused deep divisions in the Muslim community. Any division would have been detrimental to the consolidation of newly established Islamic state.

Allegiance to Abu Bakr

People swore allegiance to Abu Bakr in the Mosque of the Prophet. The choice of the first caliph was also in accordance with the usage of Arabs who decided all matters of significance through discussion and consultation. Normally, they elected "a chieftain who was ripe in age, mature in judgment, sincere and accomplished in leading the people in war and peace". [9] This old tribal custom was followed in choosing Abu Bakr for the urgency of times, which required no further delay. "It was of course not an election on the basis of adult franchise as it happens in the parliamentary form of government in our own time. Also, there was no question of any party seeking people's mandate on the basis of some programme. Neither any term of office was fixed. It was an "election" for life and with undefined powers (well within the limits of *shariah*)". [10]

Abu Bakr, by the virtue of his age and the position he had at Mecca, occupied a high place in the estimation of the Arabs. He was recognized as a man of wisdom and moderation. Ali and chief members of the Prophet's family accepted his election with their usual devotion to the faith. This particular development is highly significant for the reason that it gave no chance to the Prophet baiters to make any allegation against him over the issue of succession.

At this juncture, it is worth to note the ascension speech of Abu Bakr: "O Peoples! I have been appointed to rule over you though I am not the best among you. If I do well help me and if I do ill, correct me...Obey me as long as I obey God and His Prophet. And, if I disobey God and His Prophet, you do not owe me obedience. The weak person among you is strong before me until I have obtained for him his right and the strong person among you is weak before me until I have taken the right from him...". [11]

What Abu Bakr said was more democratic in spirit than the present day public pronouncements of the political leaders. There was no repressive machinery and this was the reason that during the reign of the first four caliphs (632-661 C.E.) we find many instances of fearless criticism of the government voiced in public. However, later on, as the caliphate changed into a dynastic rule, the repressive machinery came into existence. [12] It essentially killed the democratic spirit of Islam.

The inaugural address of the first caliph has a unique significance in Islamic history particularly at a time when everybody was interested to know as to what the caliph would say? What would be his policies and priorities? What would be the tone of his administration? Every movement of the newly chosen caliph was closely watched in the context of the gap created because of the sad demise of the Prophet. The people, because of the untimely demise of the Prophet were very much disappointed.

At the same time, they were equally excited to listen to their new leader. "Every word of (inaugural address) contains volumes of wisdom, serves as a beacon to the Muslim world. By emphasizing the fact that he would legitimately demand the obedience of his people only as long as he acted in accordance with the commands of Almighty Allah and His Prophet, Abu Bakr propounded the principle that the head of the Islamic state could never be a despot". [13]

Area under the Caliphate of Abu Bakr, 634 C.E.

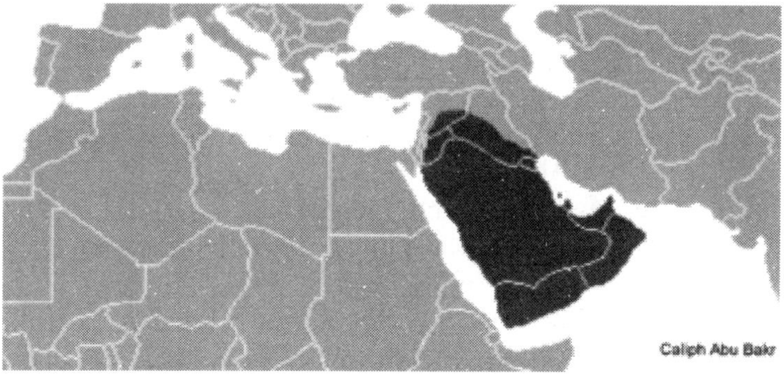

Abu Bakr is also reported to have said: "the person who has become ruler should be ready for heavy accountability and he is at the risk of heavy punishment. One who is not a ruler is less likely to be accountable and less likely to be punished. This is for the reason that rulers are more prone to torture their Muslim subjects. And he rebels against God who tortures Muslims". [14] In one of the sermons, Abu Bakr said: "(Supposing that) a person is charged with the responsibilities of the Ummah of the Prophet, the curse of Almighty Allah befalls when he does not discharge his responsibilities according to the Book of Allah". [15]

It is recorded that next day after becoming caliph, Abu Bakr, went to market carrying a bundle of clothes on his shoulder because he traded in clothes. Upon seeing this, Umar stopped him arguing that a heavy responsibility of administration has befallen on him. Umar consulted with the officer-in-charge of *bayt al maal*. He was given a stipend of four thousand dirham per year, which by the then standard was neither too high nor too low. [16] Abu Bakr conducted his official and personal affairs in such a way that he managed to return whatever he had got in allowance. "At his death he ordered that a small estate which belonged to him should be sold and the proceeds returned to the Muslim community as set-off for the sums which he had taken from them". [17] A similar narration is available in al-Daudi's *Kitab al Kharaj.* [18]

First Preference to Unity

There are conflicting reports about Ali allegiance to Abu Bakr. A few historians are of the view that, after assuming the caliphate, when Abu Bakr ascended the pulpit he did not find Ali in the Mosque of the Prophet. He sent one of the companions of the Prophet to invite Ali with the message: "O brother and son in law of the Prophet, would you like that the unity amongst Muslims should be torn to pieces? Ali sensing the gravity of situation and in broad public interest replied: "I have no grudge or complaint, O Caliph of the Prophet". With these words, Ali is reported to have sworn allegiance to him. This appears to be a sound explanation of the then situation for two reasons. First, Ali never gave up the companionship of Abu Bakr. Secondly, he never absented himself from the congregational prayers led by Abu Bakr. Ali is reported to have said: "The person with whom the Prophet of Allah was pleased (in leading prayers), we are pleased with him in our worldly affairs". [19]

This particular approach of Ali highlights one of the many glorious facets of his personality. At that particular time, Ali made it clear that the interest of Islam and the newly formed Islamic state was above all; he was free from a clannish bias; he had no hidden political agenda; he would do nothing to cause divisions in the community and that he was sincere and honest to the core. The later period events proved that he was honest to the core. His devotion to the cause of Islam remained matchless throughout his life.

Historians have recorded that immediately after the demise of the Prophet, Abu Sufyan came to Ali and Abbas and said: "Oh Ali! Oh Abbas! How it is that the caliphate has been entrusted to a clan of Quraish, lower in prestige and fewer in numbers? By God if both of you agree (to dissent) I would pack into Madinah my supporters and allies". [20] In fact, he was speaking in favour of an armed strike against the newly elected caliph. It would have been surely a highly disastrous move if Ali had accepted his advice.

This offer did not move Ali. Rejecting the same, he replied: "By God! I cannot allow you to do so. Had we not considered Abu Bakr, worthy of being caliph, we would have never allowed him to take over. Oh Abu Sufyan! The essence of faith is in integrity and truthfulness. Believers are well-wishers of one another; they love one another irrespective of the distance between them". [21] Abbas also rejected the offer and Abu Sufyan returned disappointed. To Ali, a hero of several fights, any armed strike against the newly elected caliph would not have been a difficult task. He, in the interest of unity of *ummah,* did not strike.

The movement of desertion of the faith by a few Arab tribes was another decisive factor that made Ali to realize that the unity of Muslim *ummah* was more important than any other issue. He, however, had his own perception of the then prevailing situation. Ali is reported to have commented before Abu Bakr that "we recognize your position and what God has given you, but you have taken over the leadership without our consultation. We believe that we have our share and right in the leadership, because of our relationship to the Messenger of God. Abu Bakr cried and they promised each other to meet at the Mosque at night. Ali went to the mosque and he told the people that he was not motivated in his opposition by a jealousy toward Abu Bakr or by a denial of his opposition; but we believe, he said, that we have a right in this leadership and he took it without consulting us. Thus, we felt uneasy". [22]

Nomination of Umar

Abu Bakr expired in 634 C.E. He was the caliph for only two years. He was held greatly responsible for giving a new life to the emerging state. Abdullah bin Masud, one of the companions of the Prophet is reported to have said: "After the death of the Messenger of God, we were standing on crossroad where, if Allah had not obliged in the person of Abu Bakr, it was likely that we would have been destroyed". [23] Muir writes: "But for him (Abu Bakr), Islam would have melted away in compromise with the Bedouin tribes or might have even perished in the throes of its birth". [24]

Abu Bakr nominated Umar, respected and feared by all, as the caliph. It is to the credit of Abu Bakr that in that difficult situation he made an appropriate choice. Many senior companions of the Prophet had reservations against his choice. They told Abu Bakr on his deathbed that he had appointed a harsh and rude person. Later events made it clear that Abu Bakr had made an appropriate choice. Moreover, Abu Bakr had nominated his colleague not his son or even a relative".

The short government of Abu Bakr was fully occupied with the labour of pacifying the desert tribes. It had much less time for any systematic regulation of the provinces. "But, with the reign of Umar (634-644 C.E.), a truly great man, [25] commenced that sleepless care for the welfare of the subject which characterized the early Muslim governments. Umar's accession to the caliphate was of immense value to Islam. He was a man of strong moral fiber and had a keen sense of justice, possessed of great energy and force of character...of simple habits, austere and frugal, wandering about at night to inquire the condition of the people without any guard or court...such was the greatest and most powerful ruler of the time". [26]

Umar too followed the footsteps of Abu Bakr, declaring that everybody has a right to speak about the functioning of the government. He invited people to his consultative meeting and remarked: "The purpose of inviting to you all is that you have put on me a heavy responsibility of discharging your affairs. I want that you share with me its burden. I am one among you. You are the people who testify the truth. You are free to agree or disagree with me. I don't, however, like that you follow my personal likes (and dislikes)". Exhorting the virtues of mutual deliberations and consultations, Umar remarked: "They are not good if they do not speak out and we are not good if do not accept what they say". [27]

In this context, it is interesting to note this episode. Umar once said: "By God, I do not know whether I am a king or a caliph? Someone from the audience said: "Oh Commander of Faithful! There is a great difference between a king and caliph". Thereupon, Umar enquired the difference. The man said: "The caliph is one who does not extract (money) unjustly nor he spends it unjustly and you are like that. A king on the other hand, suppresses (his people) to pay and spends whimsically". [28] He remarked that the Almighty Allah would hold him accountable if a hapless goat had died on the banks of Tigris River. [29]

He was very particular about *bayt al maal*. He once said: "I do not deserve anything more from *bayt al maal* except a pair of seasonal clothing. I should take stipend for my family, and me, which is sufficient for an average Qureshite family. I am a commoner like any other Muslim". [30] In another place, he is reported to have remarked: "So far as the public wealth is concerned, I do not consider anything right except this. It should be collected justly; it should be spent justly and its misuse should be prevented. My relation to your money is that of an orphan's guardian. I won't take anything if I do not need it. When needed I would use it in permissible limits". [31]

It was in the period of Umar that the Islamic state experienced an extraordinary territorial expansion. Under the command of Umar, his generals captured Iran, Iraq, Syria and Egypt. A total of 22,51,030 square miles area was under the rule of Umar. The flow of power, administration and justice were so well channelled that everyone felt governed. Everyone experienced adequate security, physical as well as financial. Umar's policy, in relation to himself and his family was ideal. Hundreds of millions of dirham were pouring into the treasury of the Islamic state. Though he had unlimited authority, he and his family lived in poverty. He dealt with the Muslims' treasury as the fund and trust of an orphan.

In relation to the Muslims, in general, his policy was characterized as just, firm and helpful. He sufficiently provided for the soldiers, their families and the inhabitants of Madinah and other places. As to his relations with the companions, he allotted to them according to the record of their participation in the defence of Islam. An important happening during the period of Umar was the appointment of Muawiyah as the governor of Damascus. Muawiyah's brother, Yazeed ibn Abu Sufyan, was appointed as the governor of Jordan. When Yazeed died, Umar added Jordan to the area of Muawiyah's governorate. By this, the power of Muawiyah began to grow politically and militarily. He became important enough to be feared and reckoned with.

Umar was assassinated by Firuz alias Abu Lulu on November 3, 644 C.E. at the age of 63 years. His assassin was the slave of Mughira b. Shueba. The cause of assassination was that one day he complained to Umar that his master was taxing him heavily and that the tax should be reduced. The caliph enquired how much he paid. The slave replied that he paid two dirham a day. Thereupon, the caliph asked about his profession. Firuz replied that he worked as carpenter, smith and engraver. Umar then said that in that case what he paid was not too much. This reply greatly perturbed Firuz and next day after the morning prayer, he fatally stabbed Caliph Umar.

When Umar was informed about his assassin, he thanked God maintaining: "Thank God, my assassin is not someone who has ever prostrated before God that he may altercate with me on its strength on the Day of Judgment. It was not the deed of an Arab". [32] This conveys Umar's satisfaction that no Arab was unhappy with him.

Appointment of the Council

Before Umar died, he appointed a council of six members to elect his successor. This action of Umar was in accordance with the traditions of the Prophet who remarked that the opinion of the two is better than one and the opinion of three is better than two and Allah's merciful hand is upon the collective opinion. The members of council were Usman bin Affan, Ali Ibn Abi Talib, Talha bin Ubaidullah, Zubayr bin Al-Awm, Sad bin Abi Waqqas and Abdur Rahman bin Awf. Umar had found it difficult to select any one of them in preference to the other. Several rounds of consultations were held and ultimately Usman (575-656 C.E.) was declared caliph. He was at that time 68 years old.

Area under the Caliphate of Umar, 644 C.E.

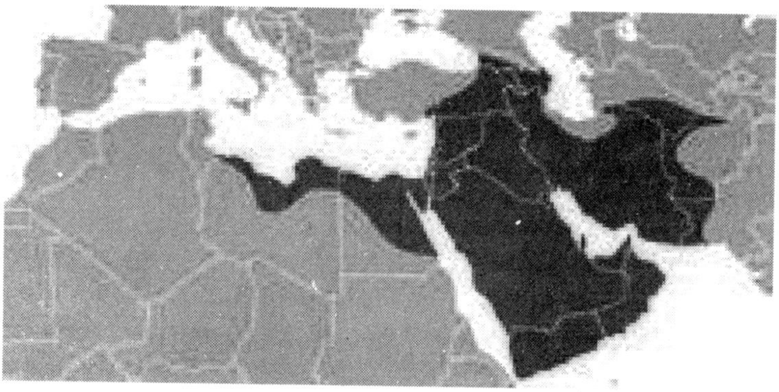

In the consultative meeting, when the choice narrowed down between Ali and Usman, Ali was asked by Abdur Rahman bin Awf: "Do you declare solemnly on my hand that you will abide by the commandments of Allah and His Apostle and follow the lead of Abu Bakr and Umar? Ali replied: "I cannot affirm that but I would try to discharge the obligations of the caliphate to the best of my ability". There was no question of not obeying the commandments of Allah and His Prophet. Ali was a little bit sceptical about the later part of the question.

Abdur Rahman left Ali and asked the same question to Usman. He replied in affirmative. Thereafter, Usman was declared as the caliph. Commenting on the refusal of Ali to repeat what was told to him, it is argued that "people were satisfied with the working of Abu Bakr and Umar and considered it as the best and most appropriate way of running the new caliphate. Therefore, Usman agreed when he asked to follow their footsteps. On the other hand, Ali being an accomplished scholar of the Quran and Sunnah of the Prophet, was competent enough to formulate his own juristic opinion hence he rejected this condition, although this would have been considered unsatisfactory by the masses". [33]

The chain of Muslim conquests continued during the period of Usman (644-656 C.E). The Islamic army acquired maritime power too. Usman did not deviate from the policy chalked out by his predecessors. However, conquests, far and wide, had brought in immense wealth and prosperity changing the way of life and social structure of the people. When Usman embraced Islam, things were different and when he became caliph, the situation had undergone a major change. The society had change from a rustic to an affluent one.

Caliphate at its Peak under Third Caliph, Usman, 656 C.E.

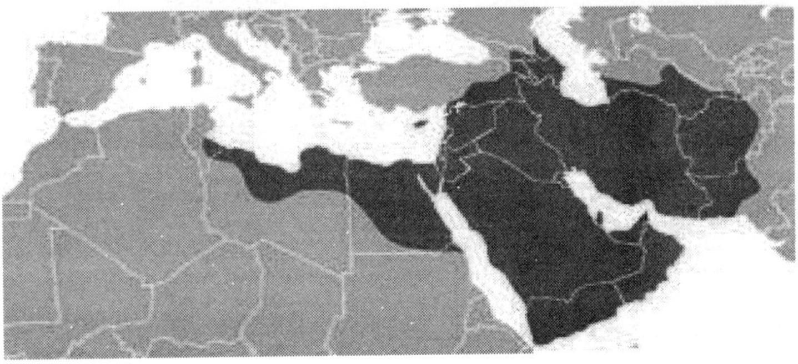

Class Formation

During the period of Umar four classes emerged and these got themselves firmly established during Usman's reign. These classes were product of historical factors. Sometimes, these cooperated with one another and at many other times contested the claims of others to serve their own interests. The four classes were: (i) the Quraysh of Mecca, (ii) the Helpers, (iii) the nomadic Arabs, and (iv) the subjects of conquered lands.

The class composition of the society changed so fast that it became increasingly difficult to reconcile different interests. This disturbed the class equilibrium. At a later stage, Ali became a victim of these developments that had drastically changed the disposition of people at large. It appears that this emergence was inevitable. "After Umar, a social crisis developed, tension was brewing between two classes of people. The first group was the Arab aristocracy, the early Muslims who had conquered these lands and had rendered services to the cause of Islam. They had thus acquired a privileged status and right in the distribution of *fai.* The second group consisted of the anonymous mass of new-Muslims, the Bedouins and disgruntled individuals at large who also wanted their share of wealth...After the changed circumstances *ummah* had reached a point where people could question the legitimacy of the system of distribution, status and privileges". [34]

Umar was a strong man and ruled with an iron hand. He rigorously imposed the Islamic morality. He meted out severe punishments to the offenders to check the corrupt practices and could dismiss many influential officers from their postings without wasting time. He succeeded mainly because there was not available any asylum to the offenders and there was no alternative power centre, as we find during the reign of Ali.

During his last days, Umar became apprehensive of changing lifestyles of the rich and reawakening of tribal loyalties. He wanted to change his policy of unequal distribution. However, his martyrdom came in the way.

It was in Syria where love of wealth plagued the people. Abu Dharr Ghiffari, one of the most contended and ascetic persons, used to reprimand people for their love of wealth. "This tendency ensured from an event that occurred during the caliphate of Usman and governorship of Muawiyah in Syria. Muawiyah asked Usman some lands out of those reserved for common people to meet his personal expenses. Following this some other officials and companions, namely Talha, Zubair, Sa'ad, Ya'li and other began keeping lands. At this preliminary stage, the implied danger of usurpation of people's right and public interest was not foreseeable. This began defeating the very purpose of Umar's ban on the ownership of land. This is why historians attach too much importance to this small beginning of a great change". [35]

Umar was a very farsighted caliph. He anticipated the shape things to come. He once told Abdullah bin Abbas while talking about his possible successors. "If I suggest Usman as my successor, he would inflict Bani Umayyah on the people and they will violate injunctions of Allah. By God if he did that, he would certainly do that and if Usman did that people would rise in revolt and kill him". [36] When Umar was on his deathbed, he called Ali, Usman and Saad bin abi Waqas and warned them saying: "After me if you happen to be the caliph, do not inflict people of your clan (as officers, governors, etc.) upon the shoulders of people". [37] Usman suffered because of the conduct of his relatives, which ultimately led to his sad assassination. The rebellion was serious and events took such a worst turn that the partiality and clannish feelings ultimately led to downfall of caliphate itself. [38]

The first four caliphs were from Quraysh. But, in case of appointment of governors of different provinces, Umar did not ignore the claims of non-Qurashites. He had even advised Usman to follow his example, but Usman ignored his advice. Many important posts were given to his relatives among Quraysh, which created hostilities among the others. During the first six years of caliphate, there was no resentment against Usman. It started developing in the last six years. [39]

Certain undesirable developments were brought to the notice of Usman. He was keen to take corrective actions. Since the circumstances were not the same as those prevailing during Abu Bakr and Umar, Usman found it difficult to reform. As the time passed, situation changed from bad to worse.

Ultimately, Usman too was assassinated on June 17, 656 C.E., at the age of 81 years. Hasan [40] reports: "I was in Madinah with Ali. We heard a loud cry. When enquired he was told that Usman is assassinated. Ali said: 'O Allah! You are my witness. I do not approve what has now happened. I was never interested (in the assassination of Usman'). He is reported to have said it for two or three times". [41]

Ali as an Advisor

The command of Ali over the interpretation of Quran and knowledge of traditions of the Prophet were universally acknowledged notwithstanding his farsightedness. There is a tradition of the Prophet describing Ali as the "gateway of knowledge". The Prophet said: "I am the city of knowledge and Ali is its gateway". [42] He was Abu Bakr's most trusted counsellor and well-wisher; always advised him what he considered to be in the interest of Islam and Muslims. [43] He never withheld his cooperation and did all he could do to strengthen the caliphate of Abu Bakr (632-634 C.E.). One such incident relates to the decision of Abu Bakr to lead the Muslim army against the apostates. He had even made necessary preparations to go to the battleground.

When Abu Bakr sat on the back of his camel, Ali took hold of the camel and said: "Where are you going Oh Caliph of the Apostle of God? I repeat what the Prophet had said on the occasion of Battle of Uhad. Sheathe you sword and depart not from us forever; if you suffer any loss, Islam will crumble to pieces forever". [44] Abu Bakr, thereupon, changed his mind. Sensing the gravity of situation and realizing the necessity of Ali, Abu Bakr in turn did not ask Ali to lead the campaign which otherwise would not have been a difficult task for Ali. Ali would have been more than pleased to push Abu Bakr into the mouth of death had the former had any grudge and bitterness against the latter.

Ali rendered his sincere advice to Umar also. In the face of Muslim expansion, the Byzantine emperor Heraclius gathered a large army, which met the Muslim army at Yarmuk in 636 C.E. It was a decisive battle in the sense that on it depended the continued possession of Syria and further advance of the Muslim army. Heraclius had come in person to Hems. Umar held a consultative meeting wherein Abdur Rehman bin Awf, along with a few other companions of the Prophet, suggested that Umar should himself lead the army to Syria.

Ali opposed the suggestion and said: "If you command this invasion personally and if you sustain a defeat or if you are killed then there will not remain any line of defence for Muslims and they shall be left without a central power to protect them. Their towns and their provinces will be left defenceless. You appoint an experienced officer to take charge of the invasion and place under him such soldiers who can face hardship, obey orders and have experience of war and if they are defeated you will be at the centre to help the Muslim state". [45] Umar dropped the idea of leading the march and remained stationed at Madinah.

Abu Ubaid adds to the above episode. Addressing Umar, Ali said that "these invaders are polytheists. They reject the monotheism. The Almighty has all the command to change (their belief from polytheism to monotheism). My advice to you is that you should ask the people of Kufa to dispatch 2/3rd of their armed personnel to fight against the invaders. The 1/3rd of defence personnel should be stationed at Kufa only to protect women and children and manage *jiziyah* administration. (Further) you should ask the people of Basra to silently keep their forces ready (for strike, if any)". [46]

Saint Sophronius (560-638 C.E.), the Patriarch of Jerusalem, negotiated the surrender of Jerusalem to Caliph Umar in 637 C.E. The Patriarch requested for peace and he put forth the condition that the Caliph himself should come in person to sign the peace treaty and taking over the keys of the city. Usman bin Aff'an expressed the view that the caliph should not go there but force the enemy to surrender more abjectly. [47] Here, Ali differed and opined that Umar must go there for this was a momentous honour, which could not be had at another occasion. He also said that this would relieve the burden on Muslims. Umar agreed to the suggestion of Ali and set out for Syria. He asked Ali to look after the affairs of Madinah in his absence. [48] Thus, from the above instances, Ali emerges as a sincere and honest advisor. When there were wars, he advised the Caliph not to leave the capital seat. When it was a peacetime, Ali impressed upon the Caliph to leave the seat and enjoy the great moment of taking over the charge of a holy city.

Similar situation arose at the time of Battle of Nahavand (642 C.E.) Umar conducted a meeting of his advisors on the issue of leading the charge. Usman bin Afaan and other companions of the Prophet advised Umar to lead the army. When asked, Ali differed from the views expressed by others. He advised that Umar should not vacate Madinah. "The position of head of the government is that of the thread for the beads as it connects them and keeps them together. If the thread were broken, they would disperse and get lost and would never come together...You should remain like the axis for them (Arabs)...Avoid battle because if you leave the place, the enemy will attack you from all sides and directions...As regards your idea about their (large) number, in the past we did not fight on the strength of large numbers but we fought on the basis of Allah's support and assistance". [49]

Ali rendered his advice in civilian and juristic matters. Umar is reported to have once remarked: "Umar would have been nowhere if Ali had not been with him". [50] Even the Prophet had recognized this quality of Ali for he is reported to have said: "Ali is most competent to solve enigmatic problems". [51] It was on the suggestion of Ali that the month of migration of the Prophet from Makkah to Madinah was taken as the beginning of Islamic calendar. Earlier to it, different methods were used to record important events and happenings.

We have already noted in the previous paragraphs that

during Umar's reign there took place a huge territorial expansion of the Islamic state. New and more fertile areas of Syria, Iraq and Persia were conquered. Consequently, there was a huge inflow of revenue in the form of war-booty. The riches, which the conquests yielded, baffled Umar. He sought some advice on the methods of dealing with the war-booty. He summoned his colleagues for their advice. Ali, keeping in view the old tribal traditions, advised him to distribute the booty to the last penny among the deserving people. At last, it was decided to prepare registers, fix daily allowances for the people and surplus was reserved for the welfare of all coming under the Islamic rule.

There is a narration reported by Na'e al-Aythi that once he entered an enclosure where camels received in *zakah* were kept. Usman was sitting in the shade writing what Ali was dictating to him. Umar was also there counting camels, giving out their colour and the number of teeth each camel had. It was a common practice then to determine the value of camels received in *zakah*. [52] This brings home a point that Ali, along with Usman and Umar, worked as an assessor or valuator of assets whenever required. There were several functionaries of *zakah* administration and assessor or valuator was one such.

Abu Ubaid reports on the authority of Harisa bin Muzarib that a few persons from Syria came to Umar. They reported that they had collected some wealth in the form of horses and slaves. They wanted to clear *zakah* dues on those items. Umar replied: "I will follow the precedence set by two of my predecessors". [53] He also consulted a few of the companions of the Prophet and Ali was one among them. Ali commented: "It is better to consider their request and allow them to clear *zakah*. But *zakah* on horses and slaves should not be made as a rule lest people after you start harassing *zakah* payers". [54] This is for the reason that during the times of the Prophet, no *zakah* was imposed on horses. This also points out that under certain circumstances, flexibility can be exercised but the same should not become a rule.

Honouring Previous Decisions

Ali not only advised Umar, as and when the need arose, he did not change certain policy decisions of his predecessors even though, after becoming caliph, he had every right to do so. Abu Ubaid, on the authority of Saalam bin Abi al-Abad, writes that once a few Christians from Najran came to Ali and complained against Umar blaming that Umar had expelled them from their lands. They requested Ali to return their lands. Thereupon, Ali remarked: "Woe to you! Umar used to deliver most appropriate decisions following all the principles of justice. I will not change his decisions". Abu Ubaid then quotes Umiash who used to say that had Ali any grudge against Umar, he would have taken it as an opportunity to reverse Umar's decisions. [55]

Further, Abu Ubaid quotes Sha'abi that when Ali made Kufa as the seat of caliphate, he declared it publicly: "I have not come here to cancel and reverse decisions made and implemented by Umar". [56] Another remark is attributed to Ali: "I have not come here to untie what has been already firmly tied down by Umar". [57] A narration similar to this is also available in al-Daudi's *Kitab al Kharaj:* "When he (Ali) arrived in Kufah, he said 'I have not come here just to undo a contract made by Umar'. The Jews submitted to Ali a letter which he had written recommending their cases to Umar. They said: 'Notwithstanding your letter and recommendations, Umar banished us'.

Thereupon Ali said: "Woe to you, Umar was rightly-guided in the matter, however, I am not going to alter any decision taken by Umar". [58] The point to note is that even though Umar had not accepted the recommendations made by Ali, when Ali became caliph and had the authority to replace previous decisions, he did not do that. Abu Ubaid quotes Ubaida narrating that Ali instructed his officials: "You decide as you used to do before. I do not like dissension. People should live and act collectively. I prefer to die as my predecessors have died". [59] This particular approach imparted much needed continuity. Ali, however, could not achieve stability.

When Ali became caliph, Banu Hashim wanted him to spend *khums* according to their interpretation, i.e., there are five shares in *khums*. But, Ali argued: "People have already interpreted and we have also interpreted, but we in our interpretation are no better than that of theirs and I do not like that Ali should be blamed for opposing the two (Abu Bakr and Umar)".

At some other place, Abu Ubaid narrates another episode on the authority of Muhammad bin Ishaq. He asked Muhammad bin Ali bin Hussain (Imam al-Baqir): "After assuming caliphate, what policy did Ali adopt in the distribution of shares to his kith and kin? Al Baqir replied: "Ali followed Abu Bakr and Umar". On being surprised, did Muhammad bin Ishaq ask: "How come? Something different used to be told". Al-Baqir replied: "By God! Ali did not like that he be blamed for opposing Abu Bakr and Umar". [60]

Reconciliation Efforts

Ali once again proved himself as a selfless advisor to Usman when disturbances emerged during the end of his caliphate. Usman asked Ali: "What are the real causes of all this disturbance and how to control it? Openly and with all sincerity, Ali replied: "Whatever is happening, it is all due to the wrong doings of your governors and high officials". Usman replied: "I have taken all the care in selecting my governors and Umar would also have done the same, then why this difference? Ali replied: "Yes it is true but Umar was a strict person and he had retained most of the powers in his own hands, everyone was afraid of his rage, even the most rebellious camel would have been terrorized by him. But, contrary to it you are a tender hearted man. Your governors are taking undue advantage of it and they are exercising their powers ruthlessly without even bringing it to your notice. The general public feels that every action, right or wrong, is being taken under your orders and hence you are considered responsible for it". [61]

When the situation turned from bad to worse, Usman came to Ali and asked him to mediate between him and his adversaries. Ali reminded him that he spoke to Usman repeatedly about certain corrective measures and the caliph, time after time, promised to take those measures. The promises remained unfulfilled by the caliph who was influenced by Marwan, Muawiyah, Abdullah ibn Saad ibn Abu Sarh.

Ali convinced Egyptians not to resort violence and on behalf of the caliph promised them to fulfil their demands. The Egyptians were demanding dismissals of Ummayyads from important administrative positions. There was also a demand to change his policy of handling the public funds. Ali went back to the caliph and advised him to go to the Mosque and pledge publicly to carry out the reform. The caliph responded positively to the good advice. He went to the pulpit and addressed the congregation saying: "I am the first one that obey God. I ask God to forgive me for what I did. I shall repent to Him...By God if justice reduces me to slave, I shall do what a slave does, and I shall be as humble as a slave. There is no escape from the anger of God but through Him. By God, I shall give you the satisfaction and I will keep Marwan and relatives away from me. I shall not separate myself from you". [62] These words moved the audience. They wept until tears moistened their beards. The caliph too wept and people hoped for good. As soon as Usman came back to his house, Marwan, his political secretary and a close relative, advised against it.

When Egyptian seized the house of Usman, Ali came to his rescue. He impressed upon them to layoff the siege but they did not relent. He remarked: "The type of siege you people have enforced around the house of Usman is not only un-Islamic; rather such disgraceful siege cannot be expected of the pagans, it is highly inhuman. When the pagans captured Muslims as prisoners, they never stopped the supplies of food and water to them". [63] The Egyptian did not care Ali and did not lift the siege. Ali became annoyed, and in protest threw his turban down on the ground and returned to his house. [64]

Ali not only advised caliphs but also the commoners as and when they approached him with their religious and juristic problems. These used to be pertaining *zakah* rates, *zakah* computation, *kharaj* payment, *jiziyah* clearance [65], etc. Abu Ubaid in his work *Kitab al Amwaal* has quoted Ali in the following narrations 1001, 1055, 1107, 1122, 1160, 1161, 1198, 1220, 1416.

Alternative Explanation

There is also available a parallel yet distinctly different explanation of Ali's role and his participation in the affairs of the then governments. [66] It is maintained that, in the first place, for almost twenty-five years, remained more or less passive. During the period of the first three caliphs (632-656 C.E.), he was sidelined in several important matters. Ali's relatively passive attitude can be better understood by comparing the active role played by him during the lifetime of the Prophet wherein he took active part in almost all expeditions alongside the Prophet. The Prophet personally took part in five battles and in all in his lifetime, twenty-seven battles were fought.

The most active and enthusiastic participant in all the enterprises in the cause of Islam and a great warrior in the forefront of all the battles fought under the Prophet, Ali reverted to leading a quite withdrawn life, almost confined to the four walls of his house. He did not take part in any of the apostasy wars, thus, still preserving his withdrawn attitude. Abu Bakr too did not ask him to participate in the wars outside Madinah. His absence can also be marked from all the wars fought under Umar. [67]

During Umar's caliphate, there were spectacular conquests of Persian and Byzantine provinces in which all the prominent companions of the Prophet took active part, Ali remained uninvolved. Nor did Ali hold any office under Umar, as had been the case under Abu Bakr and would continue later under Usman. The only exception was his holding the charge of Madinah during Umar's journey to Palestine, when he took with him all the other leading companions of the Prophet and military commanders. It was a peacetime charge. Ali alone was absent from the historic surrender of Jerusalem and Syria. Also, Umar is reported to have strictly prevented the Banu Hahsim from going out of Madinah. [68]

The rift between Ali and others did not come to the fore mainly because of fast changing circumstances. The apostasy wars during the period of Abu Bakr and conquests of foreign lands in the caliphate of Umar served the purpose of keeping the internal feuds at rest. Ali preferred public interest, which remained concealed in the unity and solidarity of Muslim community to his private interest, if any.

Moreover, the caliphate of Abu Bakr (632-34 C.E.) and Umar (634-644 C.E.) were characterized by highest levels of simplicity, justice, equality, devotion to the cause of Islam and zeal for safeguarding Muslim common interest. Despite his passive and withdrawn attitude, Ali extended, whenever sought, his advice to the earlier caliphs. His advice was sought mainly on legal matters in view of his excellent knowledge of the Quran and Sunnah. It, however, appears that he was consulted occasionally and not much advice was sought on economic issues in general and financial administration in particular.

Selection of Ali as the Caliph

After the assassination of Usman, people thronged around Ali urging him to accept the leadership of Muslims. However, Ali, noting the unfortunate events of the past and being aware of the extent of deterioration in the prevailing situation, was not disposed to accept that grave responsibility. For quite some time, a chaotic and confused situation prevailed in Madinah. For his hesitation, Ali cited three reasons: [69]

1. I am shy of the oath of allegiance from those people who

have assassinated Usman.

2. I am shy of taking allegiance because Usman's body is not yet buried.
3. I am worried about the tragedy that has befallen on all of us.

Ali was requested repeatedly to assume the charge of caliph, which he was consistently refusing. Such a situation did not exist when Abu Bakr, Umar and Usman became caliphs. It is also reported that when pressed for caliphate, Ali insisted that only *ahlul Badar* [70] (people of Badar) should elect the caliph. After sometime all *ahlul Badar* gathered and elected Ali as the caliph. [71] Nevertheless, he saw that should he reject the caliphate, the face of truth would become still more clouded, and it might be alleged that he was not interested in this matter from the very beginning, and that he gave no importance to such affairs.

When people started addressing him *Ameerul Muminin*, Ali said: "I felt greatly hurt and I prayed: 'Oh! God grant me enough courage to avenge Usman's murder so that Usman is pleased with me". [72] Ali remarked: "In order to clear doubts created by the Umayyads regarding his involvement in the murder of Usman, he was ready to clear it by taking oath fifty times between Rukan-e- Yamani and Muqam-e-Ibrahim. [73]

Moreover, the fact is that Islam does not consider it permissible for anyone to remain an idle spectator in a society divided into two classes of the oppressed and the oppressor, one suffering the pangs of hunger and the other well-fed and uneasy with the discomforts of over-eating. There was no option available to Ali but to shoulder this heavy responsibility.

He himself explains this in the sermon: "Behold, by Him who splits the grain (to grow) and created living beings, if people had not come to me and supporters had not exhausted the argument and if there had no pledge of Allah with the learned to the effect that they should not acquiesce in the gluttony of the oppressor and the hunger of the oppressed, I would have cast the rope of caliphate on its own shoulders and would have given the last one the same treatment as to the first one. Then you have seen that in my view this world of yours is not better than the sneezing of a goat". [74]

By the time Ali became caliph, the egalitarian structure of the Arabian society had been nearly shattered. Muslim society got itself divided into various groups such as Quraysh, non-Quraysh, Ansar and non-Ansar, Umayyads, non-Umayyad, Arabs, non-Arabs and so on. Their political and economic interests clashed with one another and created an unending crisis in the early Islamic society. The crisis not only resulted in civil wars, in which nearly eighty thousand Muslims died [75], but also destroyed the Islamic vision of a just and undivided democratic society. Ali could not bring forces, unleashed by the formation of different contesting classes, under control.

Ali wanted to shape his policies in accordance with the teachings of Islam, especially its egalitarian spirit by enforcing Islamic laws rigorously. "Not that these laws did not permit accumulation of wealth and private property; they did. But, nevertheless, they had laid down certain ground rules which were in the interest of Muslims as whole. These rules certainly stood in the way of those who wanted to accumulate as much as they could. Moreover, Ali was very scrupulous in the distribution of war booty. He would give equal shares to all irrespective of their status, race or region of origin. This went against the perception of groups and antagonized them. "When Ali reintroduced Umar's asceticism, they disliked the changes and were encouraged to resist by the enterprise of Muawiyah who dangled before their eyes hopes of gain". [76]

Naturally, from the very inception of Ali's reign, the elites with their hopes and expectations were disappointed. Their disappointment soon grew into subversive conspiracies against Ali's government, creating for him many a headache. Well-meaning friends, with sincere goodwill, advised Ali to adopt greater flexibility in his policies for the sake of higher interests. Their advice was: "Extricate yourself from the ruses of these demagogues, as is said, 'sewing the dog's mouth with a big morsel'. These are influential persons, some of whom are from the elite of the early days of Islam. Presently, your real enemy is Muawiyah, who is in control of a rich and fertile province like Syria.

The wisdom lies in setting aside, for the time being, the matter of equality and justice. What harm there is in it?" Ali replied to them: "Do you command me that I should seek support by oppressing those over whom I have been placed? By Allah! I won't do so as long as the world goes on and as long as one star leads another in the sky. Even if it were my property, I would have distributed it equally among them, then why not when the property is that of Allah? Beware certainly that giving of wealth without any right for it is wastefulness and lavishness. It raises its doer in this world, but lowers him in next world.

It honours him before people but disgraces him with Allah. If a man gives property to those who have not right for it or do not deserve it, Allah deprives him of their gratefulness and their love too would be for others. Then if he falls on bad days and needs their help, they would prove the worst comrades and ignoble friends". [77] This is an example of how highly Ali valued justice and equality. On these principles, he remained uncompromising all through his life.

An individual, whatever the strength of his will and character, cannot change the course of history when the tide of historical forces is against him. Ali found it extremely difficult to execute his policies and he too ultimately fell prey to the sword of an assassin. In a decisive historical struggle, Ali lost and his adversaries won, heralding an era of *mulukiat* (dynastic rule). [78] "With the establishment of Umayyad dynasty, the golden age of Muhammad and the Rightly Guided Caliphs came to an end and the caliphate became an absolute monarchy". [79]

Muawiyah (602-680 C.E.), who was governor of the

strategic province of Syria for a long-time, seized the opportunity created by the assassination of Usman. Ali knew that his Syrian governor was ambitious as well as a skilful strategist. He was appointed by Umar as the governor of Syria along with his brother Yazid bin Abu Sufiyan as the governor of Palestine. Later on when Yazid bin Abu Sufiyan expired, the area under Palestine was added to the governorship of Muawiyah. Usman continued his governorship of Syria and Palestine.

Ali, after becoming caliph, had every right to frame his own administrative policy and appoint such governors, as had full faith in his policy. Ali exercised his power against Muawiyah who had a very long and uninterrupted governorship over a large and fertile tract of land. He defied Ali and avenging Usman's murder came in as a handy issue. He wanted a plausible excuse to fight against Ali and in such circumstances, the revenge of Usman's assassination turned out to be the best one.

End Notes

1. Nizami, Khaliq Ahmad., *Some Aspects of Religion and Politics in India during Thirteenth Century,* Idarah-i-Adbiyat-i-Dilli, Delhi, 1974, pp. 1-14.
2. A later period scholar al Mawardi has made an interesting observation: "(at the time of Battle of Mutah) the Prophet appointed his manumitted slave, Zaid bin Harith, to take his place as the head of the Muslim army and at the same time ordered that in case of his death he should be replaced by Jafar bin Abi Talib, after him Abdullah bin Rawahah and in case he is also killed the mantle of command should fall on the shoulders of whomever the soldiers might choose. When it was possible for the Prophet to make these nominations, it should be possible in case of caliphate as well". The Prophet, however, preferred to remain silent. For a further discussion one may refer to Haroon Khan Sherwani's *Muslim Political Thought and Administration*, Munshi Ram Manoharlal Publishers Pvt. Ltd., 1981, p. 80.
3. Khuda Baksh S., *Politics in Islam,* Idarah-i-Adabiyat-i-Delli, Delhi, 1981, reprint, pp. 7-8.

4. Khuda Baksh S., *Politics in Islam,* op.cit., p. 8.
5. Esposito, John L., *Islam the Straight Path*, Third Edition, Oxford University Press, 1998, p. 38.
6. Nadwi, S.A.A., *The Life of Caliph Ali,* op. cit., pp. 54-55. A similar discussion is also available in Shah Waliullah Muhadith Dehlvi's *Izalatul Khulfa,* op. cit. and in *al-Budur al-Bazigah,* Kitab Bhavan, New Delhi, 1997, pp. 79-81, 92-93, 97-98.
7. For a detailed history of caliphate, one may refer to Jalaluddin Suyutis' *Tarikh al Khulfa,* (Urdu), Farid Book Depot Pvt. Ltd., Delhi, 2004. Its English translation is also available.
8. Sherwani, op. cit., p. 115.
9. Nadavi, S.A.A., *The Life of Caliph Ali,* op. cit., p. 70.
10. Engineer, Asghar Ali, *The Islamic State*, Vikas Publishing House Pvt. Ltd., New Delhi, 1980, p. 36.
11. Sherwani, Muhammad Habibur Rahman Khan., *Life of Abu Bakr: The First Caliph of Islam,* (3rd Edition), Adam Publishers and Distributors, Delhi, p. 40. See also, Atta Mohy-ud-din's *Abu Bakr,* S. Chand & Co., New Delhi, 1968, pp. 17-18; Muhammad Husayn Haykal's *Siddiq-e-Akbar* (Urdu) 2nd Edition, Islamic Book Foundation, New Delhi, 1999.
12. For a systematic analysis of caliphate turning into a dynastic rule, one may refer to S.A.A. Moududi, *Khilafat wa Malukiat,* Markazi Makatab-e-Islami Publishers, New Delhi, 2008.
13. Sherwani, Muhammad Habibur Rahman Khan, *Life of Abu Bakr: The First Caliph of Islam,* op. cit., p. 40.
14. *Kanz al-ummal: Vol. No. 6,* Narration No.78.
15. *Kanz al-ummal: Vol. No.6,* Narration Nos. 293, 294, 295, 296, 299, 301.
16. *Kanz al-ummal*: *Vol No. 5*, Narration Nos. 2280-2285; SAAM, p. 74. Jurji Zayadan reports that it was 6,000 dinars. Please refer to Jurji Zayadan's *History of Islamic Civilisation: Umayyads and Abbasids*, translated into English by D.S. Margoliouth, Kitab Bhavan, 2006.
17. Zayadan Jurji, *History of Islamic Civilisation: Umayyads and Abbasids*, op. cit., p. 37.
18. Al-Daudi, *Kitab al Kharaj*, Islamic Research Institute, Islamabad, Pakistan, 1995, pp. 112-113.
19. *Tarikhul Khulfa,* p. 93.
20. Nadwi, S.A.A., *The Life of Ali,* op.cit., p. 80.
21. op.cit.

22. Chirri, Muhammad Jawad, *The Brother of Prophet Mohammad*, Ansariyan Publications, Qum, Iran, 1996, p. 190.
23. Baladhuri, *Futuh al Buldan.,* Urdu translation by Sayed Abulkhair Maududi, Vol. 1, Hyderabad, 1932, pp. 150-151.
24. Muir, Sir William., *Annals of Early Caliphate,* quoted by Sayed Athar Hussain, in *The Glorious Caliphate,* Academy of Islamic Research and Publication, Lucknow, 1974, p. 19.
25. Umar became caliph at the age of 52 years.
26. Nadvi, S.A.A., *The Life of Caliph Ali,* op. cit., p. 95.
27. For a detailed account of life and times of Umar, one may refer to Shibli Numani's magnum opus, *Al-Farooq,* Naaz Book Depot, Delhi. Its English translation is also available.
28. *Tarikhul Khulfa*, p. 220.
29. *Kanz al Ummal: Vol. No. 5,* Narration No. 2512.
30. *Tabaqat ibn Saad, Vol. No. 3*, pp. 306-307.
31. *Kanz al Ummal: Vol. No.5,* Narration Nos. 2280-2285.
32. Nadvi S.A.A., *The Life of Caliph Ali,* op. cit., p. 107.
33. Nadvi S.A.A., *The Life of Caliph Ali,* op. cit., p. 132.
34. Haque, Ziaul, *Landlord and Peasant in Early Islam,* Islamic Research Institute, Islamabad, Pakistan, Reprint, 1984, p. 231.
35. Amini, Muhmmad Taqi, *Agrarian System in Islam*, Idarah-e-Adbiyat-e-Dilli, Delhi, 1991, p. 95. Esposito, John L., *Islam The Straight Path*, op. cit., p. 39.
36. Moududi, Sayed Abu Ala, *Khilafat wa Malukiat*, op. cit., p. 82 on the authority of Ibn Abdl al- Barr *Al-Istiab.*
37. Moududi SAA., *Khilafat wa Malukiat.,* op. cit., p. 83.
38. Ibid.
39. *Tarikh ul Khulfa,* pp. 231-252.
40. Eldest son of Ali who was poisoned at the age of 47 years.
41. *Kanz ul Um'mal,* Narration No. 36313.
42. *Tarikhul Khulfa* on the authority of Tirmizi and Hakim, p. 257.
43. Nadavi, S.A.A., *The Life of Caliph Ali,* op. cit., p. 81.
44. Ibid.
45. *Nahjul Balagha:* Sermon Nos.137, p. 260 and 149, p. 270.
46. *Kitba al Amwal,* Narration No. 622.
47. Nadvi, S.A.A., *The Life of Caliph Ali,* op. cit., p. 101.
48. Ibid.
49. Nadvi, S.A.A., *The Life of Caliph Ali*, op. cit., p. 100.
50. Nadvi, S.A.A., *The Life of Caliph Ali,* op. cit., p. 97.
51. Ibid.

52. Nadvi, S.A.A., *The Life of Caliph Ali,* op. cit., p. 96.
53. In fact, Umar is referring here the Prophet who passed away in the year 632 C.E. and Abu Bakr who passed away in 634 C.E.
54. *Kitab al Amwal,* Narration No. 1364.
55. *Kitab al Amwal,* Narration Nos. 273, 274 and 275.
56. *Kitab al Amwal,* Narration No. 275.
57. *Kitab al Amwal,* Narration No. 848.
58. Al-Daudi Abu Jafar Ahmad ibn Nasr., *Kitab al Amwal,* Islamic Research Institute, Islamabad, Pakistan, 1995, p. 55.
59. *Kitab al Amwal,* Narration No. 849.
60. *Kitab al Amwal,* Narration No. 847.
61. Nadvi, Shah Moinuddin, *Hazrat Ali Al Murtuza*, Idara Isha'at-e-Diniyat (P) Ltd., New Delhi, 1997, pp. 37-38. The author has quoted from *Jami' Al-Tabri.* p. 2938.
62. Ibn al-Atheer, *Al-Kamil,* Part 3, Dar Al-Kitab Al-Lubnani, 1973, p. 82.
63. Ibne Atheer quoted by Shah Moinuddin Nadwi, *Hazrat Ali Al-Murtuza,* op. cit., p. 40.
64. Ibid.
65. Khaliq Ahmad Nizami writes that *jiziyah* is an Arabicised form of Persian word *gezit* which means a tax. It was known long before the advent of the Prophet of Islam. Nausherwan had formulated rules about it. According to Tabari, Nausherwan fixed this tax as the rate of 12, 8, 6, 4 dirhams per capita but exempted all: (a) high born people, (b) nobles, (c) military men (d) religious leaders, (e) scholars, (f) courtiers, and (g) persons under 20 years of age from the payment of this tax. It was realized by him in lieu of exemption from military services. When the Prophet of Islam imposed this tax, after giving it the Arabic form of jiziyah, he followed a tradition established long before him. The second caliph, Umar followed the same tradition. For further details one may refer to Khaliq Ahmad Nizami's *Some Aspects of Religion and Politics in India During the 13th Century,* op. cit., pp. 310-311.
66. Werner Ende, " Shi'i Islam", in Werner Ende and Udo Steinbach (eds.) *Islam in the World Today,* Cornell University Press, Cornell, 2010, pp. 51-69.
67. Jafri, S.H.M., *The Origin and Early Development of Shia Islam,* Oxford University Press, Karachi, Pakistan, 2000, pp. 59-61.
68. Jafri, S.H.M., *The Origins and Early Development of Shia Islam,*

op. cit., p. 65.

69. *Tarikhul Khulfa*, p. 249.
70. People of Badar means those companions of the Prophet, who alongside the Prophet, took part in the Battle of Badar in 2 A.H. (624 C.E.).
71. *Tarikhul Khulfa,* p. 246.
72. Ibid.
73. *Kanz ul ummal,* Narration No. 36312; Rukun-e-Yamani.the southwest corner of Kaaba is known as Rukan-e-Yamani since it faces Yeman...Muqam-e-Ibrahim is a place in the precincts of Kaaba where prayer is offered.
74. *Nahjul Balagha,* Sermon No. 3, New York Edition.
75. Heribert Busse, "The World of Islam: A Brief Historical Survey", in Werner Ende and Udo Steinback (eds.), *Islam in the World Today,* Cornell University Press, Cornell, 2010, pp. 13-14.
76. Zayadan, Jurji, *History of Islamic Civilisation: Umayyads and Abbasidd*, op. cit., p. 39.
77. *Nahjul Balagha*, NY, p. 279, Sermon No. 125.
78. Nizami, Khaliq Ahmad, *Some Aspects of Religion and Politics in India During the Thirteenth Century*, op. cit., p. 19.
79. Esposito, John L., *Islam the Straight Path*, Third Edition, Oxford University Press, 1998.

3

Values Personified

The Personal Approach of Ali

The personal approach has a great bearing upon the way in which a person conducts himself, publicly as well as privately and how he manages affairs individually as well as collectively. "The beliefs and values held strictly, cherished and revered by a family get in-built in the minds of the people belonging to it and any one disregarding them is considered as the rebel and a renegade not to be tolerated by others (of the same family)". [1] Similarly, inherited traits are also generally visible in the stature, appearance, intonation, etc. Abu Huraira relates from the Prophet: "People are mines, like those of silver and gold. Those among them who were distinguished in the day of ignorance will also be outstanding after entering into the fold of Islam". [2]

Long before he became caliph, Ali had defeated a powerful foe in the battle and was about to kill him, the latter spat on his face. Ali immediately got off his chest and let him go. This greatly surprised him. Upon this, Ali replied: "If I had killed you after you spat on me, it would have been an act of revenge" and revenge killing is not a religious act.

The personal approach of Ali is clear from the following instance as reported by Suyuti. [3] He also comments that the whole narration is authentic. "Once Umar climbed on the pulpit to address the gathering. Hussain, son of Ali, was also present there. When he saw Umar on the pulpit, Hussain asked him to get down maintaining that the pulpit was of his grandfather. Umar asked: 'The pulpit is definitely of your grandfather and it does not belong to my father. But please tell who prompted you to ask this question? Ali, who was present in the gathering, immediately stood up and said: 'By God! I have never instigated Hussain'. He reprimanded Hussain. Thereupon Umar told: "Do not scold my nephew. He is right. This pulpit is of his grandfather only". This episode makes it clear that Ali never abused or expressed his displeasure against Umar even when he was in private with his family members. The family members in general and children in particular learn many things from their elders and occasionally disclose the same in public.

In the battle of Siffin [4] (657 C.E.) Ali recaptured river Euphrates from Muawiyah. Earlier, Muawiyah and his army did not allow Ali's army to take water from the river when it was under their control. It was now Muawiyah's turn to beseech permission to get water. Ali's army personnel told him that the very people had refused water to them, why should they be allowed to take water? Ali replied: "They are human beings and though have acted inhumanly yet I cannot allow (to follow) their example and cannot refuse food and water because he (Muawiyah) happens to be my worst enemy". [5]

In the battle of Nahrwan, [6] (657 C.E.) Ali was fighting like any other ordinary soldier. A soldier from the rival party came to fight against Ali, and in the encounter, he lost his sword. Ali realised his hopeless plight and asked him to run away saying: "Flee Oh Friend! You are not in a position to defend yourself". This attitude of Ali made his opponent bolder. He said: "Why do not you kill me, it would have made one less for you". Ali replied: "I cannot strike a man who cannot defend himself. You were begging for your life and it was spared". The opponent got still bolder and said: "I am told that you have never refused a beggar. Now I beg you of your sword, will you give it to me? Ali gave his sword. Taking possession of the sword, the opponent said: "Now Ali! Who is going to defend you against me and save you from my killing blow? Ali replied: "Of course God! He will defend me if he so wills. He has appointed my death to be my guarding angel, none can harm me before it is due and none can save me when it arrives".

This magnanimous reaction of Ali impressed his opponent so much that he kissed the bridle of Ali's horse and said: O lord! You are a great man indeed. You not only forsake the life of your enemy in the battlefield but you also gift him your sword. May I have the honour to act as your bodyguard and fight for you? Ali replied: "Friend! Fight for the truth and justice and do not fight for persons". [7]

A Graphical Account

Dharar bin Dhamurah presented a graphical account of Ali's personality before Muawiyah in these words: "He was very far-sighted, very strong, inclined to stoutness, candid in speech and absolutely just in delivering a verdict. He was the fount of knowledge and looked askance at the world and its pleasures. The night and its darkness were more agreeable to him. God be my witness that his eyes were often filled with tears and he always appeared to be care-worn. He had the touch of conscience, which often made him to reproach himself. He was happy to wear garments made of coarse cloth and to partake coarse food, lived like a common man and made no distinction between himself and others.

Whenever we asked anything, he replied, whenever we went to see him, he saluted first and whenever we invited him, he came ungrudgingly. Despite his nearness, his awe seldom permitted us to talk in his presence or join in his conversation. Whenever he laughed his teeth used to shine as hailstones. He respected the pious and loved poor. No man of influence or authority could hope to achieve any undeserved gain from him, nor did the weak ever give up hope obtaining justice from him. I declare to God that I have seen him often after the nightfall, standing on a prayer mat holding his beard and weeping bitterly. I have heard him sobbing and lamenting. It seemed as if a scorpion or snake had stung him. I can still visualise him saying: "Oh world! Dost thou want to entice me away? Hast thou brought thy charms for me? Away, away with thee.

Go about the business and deceive somebody else. I have

already divorced thee thrice. O world! Thy pleasures are transitory, thy life is short and thy allurements are unreliable and dangerous. Alas! I have put little provisions, the voyage is long and the route is extremely perilous". [8] When asked about his separation, following the martyrdom, Dharrar replied: "My grief is comparable to the woman whose child has been slain in her lap, whose tears neither dry nor her grief is lightened". [9]

There is a narration in al-Daudi's *Kitab al-Kharaj* which portraits the personality of Ali. "Ali was moderate in dress and food. He had inclination towards coarse cloth; and he used to cut both of his sleeves at the upper end of the sides of this fingers. He used to walk on foot through mud or rain and disposed of all that was in his *bayt al-maal* every Saturday. [10] Whenever he looked at the contents of the *bayt al maal,* he said: 'This is my collection which comprises the best of it. O red (gold) [11] o white (silver), you deceive everyone save me'. When he died nothing was found in his possession except three hundred dirham which he had arranged for buying a slave". [12]

Portrayal in *Nahjul Balagha*

A study of different sermons of Ali contained in *Nahjul Balagha* (lit. *Peak of Eloquence*) will be of great help in understanding his personal approach. From the contents of *Nahjul Balagha*, Ali appears to be a man of many parts. As an administrator, Ali was neither an autocrat nor a weakling. Like a democrat, he believed in consultations. He preferred peace to war and even during wartime never attacked first. He was open to corrections as is clear from one of his letters. "I am leaving this city either as a tyrant and as an oppressor or I am being tyrannised and oppressed; either I am revolting against the people or some of them have intrigued to revolt against me. Whatever the case may be I invite in the name of God to those to whom letter reaches to come and see for themselves whether I am right or the wrong. If they find me on the path of truth and justice they may help me and if they find that I am on the wrong path, they can reason me out of it". [13]

His choice of team of officers and administrators reflects the sincerity of purpose. The only characteristic, which Ali lacked, was opportunism and unscrupulousness. His failures, if there were, can be attributed to this and to the fear of God and love for Islam, which often withheld him from taking a wrong, hasty and short-sighted stand. He was a fervent Muslim, honest both in speech and in action, unacquainted with crooked ways and tricks. His sole concern was religion and the basis of all his actions was the truth.

Ali strictly followed the principle of equality. To him all were Muslims and he never showed preference to any one because of relation, race, clan or tribe. It is not out of place to quote an instance here. One-day two women came to Ali and explained their needs. Upon this, food grains and some clothes were purchased and distributed equally between the two. One of them, however, said that she should be given more because she was Arab and her colleague a non-Arab. Ali took some soil in his hand and looking at it he said: "I do not know if God has given preference to someone over the other except on grounds of piety and obedience to him". [14]

Asceticism and Piety

Numerous anecdotes are on record illustrating the asceticism and piety of Ali. [15] Ibn Shihab says: "An ascetic is one in whom neither the lawful things exhaust his gratitude (for Allah) nor do the prohibited things exhaust his patience". [16] "He was a fervent Muslim, free both in speech and in action, unacquainted with crooked ways and unable to employ ruses. His sole concern was religion and basis of his action was truth. As an illustration of his bare minimum living, it is recorded that when he married Fatimah, the Prophet's daughter, they had no bed save a ram's skin to lie at night and feed their camel from it the daytime. He wore tunic too thin to protect him from cold". [17]

Here only those events are identified which are directly related to his economic approach, wisdom and philosophy. For example, when he was the caliph some money came to him from Isfahan; this he divided into seven portions, and, as a loaf of bread remained over, he divided that too into seven portions. [18] Once a dish full of sweet was brought to him. Ali said: "Its colour is bright, taste is better, its fragrance is sweet. But I do not like it. I do not want to addict myself with the things I do not approve". [19]

On an occasion, a group of persons claiming to be his followers came to Ali's doorsteps. Ali enquired from Qumnbar [20] as to who these people were? He told Ali that they claimed to be his followers. Ali was surprised and said: "I do not see any trait that they are my followers". An equally surprised Qumnbar said: "Oh my master! What are the traits (of your followers)? Ali replied "Pinched with famine, dry with thirst and blear-eyed with tears". [21]

Once he was carrying a dirham's worth of dates that he had bought, in a wrapper. Some from his subjects offered to carry them for him; he replied that his was the duty of the *paterfamilias*. Whenever he sent soldiers on expeditions, he urged them to deal gently with the enemy, and particularly to see that no harm befell the women. When Obaidullah ibn Abbas, as the governor, ill-treated the Bani Tameem clan, Ali wrote: "You should not behave like beast with your subjects. They are respectable people and should be treated respectfully. You are representing me and your treatment is considered as that of mine. Your first consideration should be the welfare of those over whom you rule and then to treat them with due respect and consideration". [22]

Ali excelled in self-discipline in his personal expenditure. He was not unaware of the caliph's right to the subsistence from *bayt-al-maal* but he voluntarily gave up his share. He sold his sword in the market to buy a shirt. When some of his associates found him shivering in the cold they advised him to get a woollen blanket from the *bayt-al-maal* but he choose to forgo it. [23] Abu Ubaid reports that a few of his colleagues impressed upon Ali that he and his family members have their right over *bayt al maal*. Ali refused their advice maintaining that he did not want to put pressure upon *bayt al maal*. [24] Ibn Abee Rafay reports that Ali used to take very simple food. He asked: "Has God prohibited you to eat better food? He replied: "No, but I want to eat the kind of food which the poorest of my realm can afford at least once a day. I shall improve it after I have improved their standard of life. I want to live, feel and suffer like them".

His contemporaries regarded Ali's conduct as his personal weakness and his partisans gradually deserted him. The following is a typical case and an apt commentary upon the conduct of some of his men of affairs. Masqalah ibn Hubayrah ash-Shaybani was Ali's governor of Ardashir Khurrah (a city in Iran). There was some revolt, which was crushed by Maq'il. He took with him those Christians of Bani Najiyah who had taken part in the revolt together with their families. These prisoners wailed and cried before governor Masqalah. He purchased prisoners from Maq'il for five hundred thousand dirham. He paid some amount and promised to pay remaining at the earliest. Ali waited for the remaining payment, which did not come.

When Ali insisted for the remaining payment, Masqalah deserted Ali and joined the ranks of Muawiyah who made him the governor of Tabarastan. Masqalah commented: "if it had been Hind's son (Muawiyah) he would not have demanded payment, and if it had been Usman Ibn Affan, he would have presented him (Masqalah) with the whole sum".

During the battle of Siffin (657 C.E.), a man came forward to address the opponents of Caliph Ali and inquired in a tone of astonishment if Ali had misused *fai*? They said never did he misuse and mismanage public funds. Then he asked what for the war? There was long silence and no reply. Uways al-Qarani, is generally regarded as the greatest of *Taibun*. He fought for Ali in the battle of Siffin and was martyred. [25]

Ali had two slaves. One was Qumnbar and the other was Saeed. Ali never got angry with them, let alone whipping or beating. Once and only once, however, Ali lost his cool. It was the occasion when Qumnbar showed him the money he had saved along with certain gifts. The money was from Qumnbar share from public treasury. The members of household of Ali presented gifts to Qumnbar. Since he had no immediate use of it, therefore, the amount got accumulated.

On seeing this, Ali was annoyed and saddened. Qumnbar enquired as to why he was so sad? Ali said: "Qumnbar, if you had no use of this money, were there not people around you who were in need of it, some of them might have been starving and some ill and infirm, could you not have helped them? I never thought that you could be so heartless and cruel and could love wealth for the sake of wealth. Qumnbar I am afraid you are not trying to acquire much from Islam, try more seriously and sincerely. Take these coins out of my house". Sensing the mood of his master, Qumnbar took his entire balance and distributed amongst the beggars in and around the Kufa mosque.

A slightly different version is available from Abu Ubaid's *Kitab al Amwal.* On the seeing the accumulation, Ali reprimanded Qumnbar and remarked: "Let your mother weep for you. You have brought fire in the house". Immediately Ali got it weighed and distributed amongst needy and deserving. He commented: "Oh wealth of this world I will not come under your lure. Go somewhere and entice others". [26] On some other occasion, when heaps of gold and silver were arranged, Ali remarked: "Oh the wealth! You cannot delude me, try others". [27]

Ali was very much disturbed when Abu Dharr Ghifari was deported from Madinah for holding extreme views pertaining to the ownership of wealth and its unequal distribution. [28] Ali was not an extremist but was against concentration of wealth in a few hands. He commented: "O Abu Dharr! People are afraid of you because they will lose their worldly possessions and positions and you are afraid of them because you thought that Islam would suffer on their account". [29] This remark of Ali was a comment on the rot that had spread in the Muslim civil society by that time.

On the issue of distribution of wealth, there arose a violent dispute between Abu Dharr and Muawiyah who sent him to the caliph as a fomenter of discord and strife. The caliph in turn deported him to a small village of Rabadah. [30] In *Tadkhirah of Hamdun,* the following is related about Abu Dharr: "When Muawiyah built his green palace at Damascus he asked Abu Dharr what he thought of it. He replied: "If thou hast built it with public money thou art a traitor, if with thy own thou art a squanderer". [31]

Extreme Simplicity

Ali favoured neither ostentatious living nor the life of a hermit. In case of commoners, he favoured moderation and for the men of affairs his advice was to practice extreme simplicity. This is clear from the following event. Once one of his companions, Ala bin Ziyad al Harisi fell ill. He went to his house and found it spacious and big. Upon this, Ali asked: "What are you going to do with such a spacious house in the world? What you really require is a spacious abode in the Heaven where you are going to stay permanently. If you sincerely desire to own also a house there along with this and as big as this one then make this house a centre of your hospitality, treat your relatives well, go to their help, be particular in doing you duties...".

Al-Harisi requested Ali to advise his brother, Aasim, who wearing coarse clothes had started leading the life of a recluse. He spoke to Aasim: "O enemy of yourself, devil has misled you. Do you not feel pity on your wife and children and other members of your family? What do you think that God will get angry with you if you eat, consume and use all those things which have been allowed by Islam and which you have earned with honest and pious means? Why renounce all that? After gathering necessary courage, Aasim replied: "Oh *Ameerul Mumineen*! I am following your example. Look at your dress how coarse, rough and cheap it is! Even our poorest will not care to wear it. Look at your food, it is dry and stale, bread not obliged to a pinch of salt even". Upon this comment, Ali replied: "Alas friend you are mistaken. You are not like me. God has made incumbent upon honest and just rulers to keep themselves on the level of poorest and humblest of men so that those people may not feel ashamed and humiliated on account of their condition. They should not lose their heart, should not give in to frustration and grief and should maintain their self-respect". [32]

Some one invited Usman bin Hunaif, one of the trusted companions of Ali and the governor of Basra province, for dinner. When Ali came to know of this, he immediately wrote a letter expressing his displeasure in clear words. "I am sorry to hear the news. I never expected that you would accept invitation of persons who invites high officers and rich people and from whose door poor persons and hungry paupers are turned away rudely...Look at your *imam* (how he conducts himself). In this world, he has satisfied himself and is content with two old torn coarse garments and two pieces of bread (one in the morning and one in the evening). I know that to adopt such a hard way of life is beyond you but at least try to be pious. Try to follow me and be my companion in virtue, piety and simple living. Oh ibn Hunaif! Fear God and be content with the bread that you get with lawful means so that you may be exempted and freed from the fire of hell". [33]

Unparalleled Care for Justice

Ali is known for his unparalleled care for justice. It happened that once Ali lost his cuirass. [34] After sometime, he saw that that a Christian was selling the same in a market. Ali, being a caliph, did not snatch the same immediately nor did he use force thereafter. Instead, he filed a case in the court of local *qazi*. The *qazi* dismissed Ali's plea because of insufficient evidence. The conduct of Ali and his Qazi impressed the Christian so much that he immediately embraced Islam. In turn Ali presented him the cuirass as well as a horse. It is said that he fought alongside Ali in the battle of Nahrwan (657 C.E.) against *Kharijites* and achieved martyrdom.

In another case when Ali appeared before a local qazi, the latter stood up as a mark of respect. Ali immediately admonished him saying: "It is justly unjust". [35] Ali is reported to have advised Shareeh, his chief *qazi,* in these words: "So long you do not speak, your tongue is your slave. You became its slave once you start speaking. Listen (it is important to note that) what are you deciding, about whom you are deciding and how you are deciding". [36]

There is another narration that a person came to Ali from a far-off place. Ali treated him as a guest and served him food. After the food was over, the visitor said that he wanted to put before Ali his lawsuit. Upon this, Ali asked him to leave the place at once and said: "The Prophet of Allah has forbidden us to treat as the guest one party to the lawsuit while ignoring the other party". [37]

Once, during the terminal days of his caliphate, a few seceders *(kharijites)* were arrested. They were brought before Ali. Upon their arrival, they started abusing Ali on his face in filthiest language. One was swearing in the name of God to assassinate Ali. Ali did not put them behind bars on the contrary released them. He addressed his companions: "You may, in retaliation, abuse them, using equally filthy language. Abusing is not that serious a crime. I will not punish them until they (harm me) by their rebellious attitude". Abu Ubaid on the authority Kasee bin Namr cites similar episode. He reports that Ali said that we have three obligations in respect of these *kharijites,* (i) we will not prevent them from offering prayers in the mosques, (ii) so long as they support us, we will allow for them a share in *fai'* and (iii) we will not declare war against them until they attack us. [38] Abu Ubaid comments that Ali approved *kharijites'* share in *fai* even though they used filthy language against Ali. They continued to create problems and made things difficult for Ali. [39] Ultimately, a *khariji* only assassinated Ali.

The Period of Ali (656-661 C.E.)

After the martyrdom of Usman, there was no caliph for three days. There was utter disorder and bewilderment. People requested Ali to assume caliphate, which he refused maintaining that this was not the method. "This is the responsibility of *ahle shura* and *ahle Badr*". Upon the persistent insistence from *muhajirun* and *ansar*, Ali agreed and went to *Masjidun Nabi* where people took oath of allegiance in public as he was against the oath of allegiance in private. He wanted it to be a public affair. [40] A report says: Ali came to the mosque clad in wrapping and a woollen turban. He had his shoes in his hand. Leaning on his bow, he ascended the pulpit and received the oath of fealty from people". [41] *Musnad Ahmad* reports that after the assassination of Usman, Ali said: "Compared to others I deserve to be made a caliph. I rose to the occasion. Now God alone knows whether I have taken a proper decision or not". [42]

First Sermon

Ali was proclaimed as the fourth caliph on Friday, June 24, 656 C.E. Before the oath of allegiance, a survey of public opinion was made in Madinah. "Everybody opined that no one except Ali was competent to hold that precarious office. In fact nobody was left thereafter Abu Bakr, Umar and Usman who had the ability and competence of Ali to hold the helm of Islamic empire at the crucial state". [43] Ali became the first and only caliph in whose selection a great majority of the community took an active part. The events also made it clear that Ali did not forcibly seek oath of allegiance nor did he ever attempt to usurp the caliphate.

Area under the Caliphate of Ali, 661 C.E.

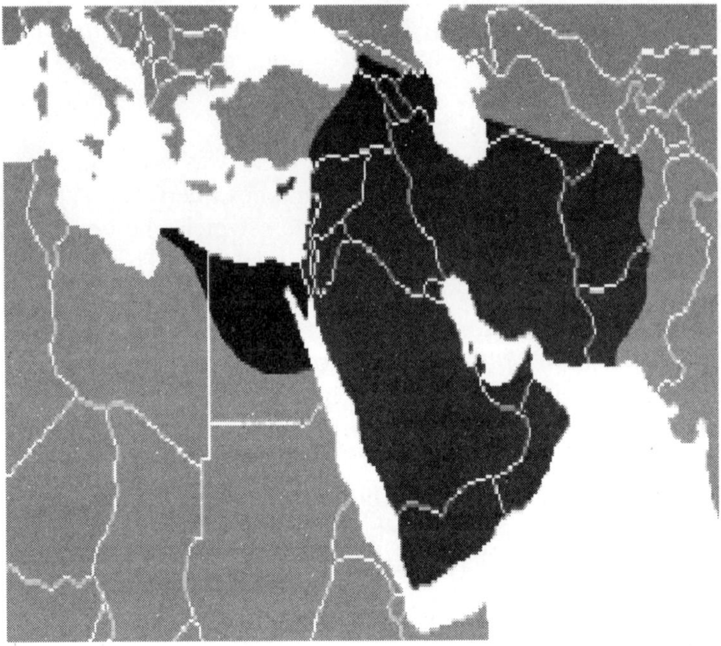

[Regions under the control of Muawiyah (red), Amr ibn al-'As (blue), and Ali (green) during the first Islamic civil war].

Let us now turn to the first sermon of Ali as the caliph. The time of Friday prayer arrived. He made use of it for delivering his first public address. He spoke: "Allah has sent down His Book as the Guide which elucidates the good and the evil; so adopt the good and eschew the evil. Allah has made many things inviolable; of these, the highest is the (life of a) Muslim... He (alone) is a Muslim from whose hands and tongue all other Muslims are safe...It is not good for any Muslim to put other Muslim to harm save that it becomes mandatory to do so.

Make haste to discharge the obligations you owe to the commoners and the elites both. The people are in your front and Doomsday behind you. It is approaching fast; keep yourself light so that you reach your destination...Fear God in fulfilling your obligations to the creations of God and their habitations. You will be questioned about the beasts and the land (on the Day of Judgement). I ask you again to obey Allah and keep away from His disobedience and sins. Adopt if you find anything virtuous; avoid if you find an evil". [44]

This first address of Ali is a fine blend of worldly and otherworldly responsibilities of both rulers and ruled. He asks people to adopt the good and eschew evil. In fact, he is referring to the famous verses from Quran which invite faithful to do good and forbid evil (3:104, 110, 114; 5: 78-79). He impresses upon all to be dutiful otherwise they would be taken to the task on the Day of Judgement. Ali conveys a message that he is not interested in any bloodshed. He is interested in the welfare of his people, their lands and animals grazing on them. "The blood of Muslims had been rendered so cheap that Caliph Usman had to become the victim of their insurgency.

This calamity had befallen in Madinah near the grave of the Prophet and in his own mosque in the presence of Muslims. Therefore, it was incumbent for the successor of departed caliph to dwell upon the inviolability of Muslim life and blood in his first address...". [45] From this observation of Ali, it is clear that he was very particular about the sanctity of the place where the Prophet is buried; the mosque and the city of the Prophet and the human blood.

In one of the sermons, Ali, as the caliph, remarked: "It is a duty of the ruler of the Muslims to rule according to the law of Almighty and be truthful to them. While he is doing so, it a duty of subjects to obey and listen to him. They should respond to his call whenever such a call is made". [46] On some other occasion, he said: "Being faithful to Allah, whenever I order you, you have to accept my command whether you like or dislike it. If I happen to be unfaithful to Allah and order you to obey me, your obedience to me then is not a compulsion". He then repeated for three times: "Obedience is only in righteousness; obedience is only in righteousness; obedience is only in righteousness". [47]

In letter and spirit, the first sermon of Ali is very much similar to those of Abu Bakr and Umar. He and his predecessors held caliphate as a "trust" and as the "trustees" they governed the people according the laws of Almighty. Ali impresses upon the people that, when people are governed according to laws of Almighty, they should obey the caliph because in the obedience of caliph is concealed the obedience of Allah. Ali further qualifies the obedience by tagging the same to the righteousness, which is repeated for three times.

Genesis of the Problems

From the very start, Ali inherited great problems which none of his three predecessors had had to face. [48] First, because of certain developments, the assassins of Usman remained outside the control of Ali. Secondly, a few of prominent companions of the Prophet, numbering 17 or 20, did not take oath of allegiance. Their non-cooperation greatly confused whole situation and added to the difficulties that Ali was already facing. Each of them was an influential person and enjoyed trust of great many number of people.

Had they strengthened the hands of Ali, things would have taken a different course. It was possible to avoid bloodshed. Thirdly, two different groups, rose against Ali, demanding revenge of Usman's murder. One group comprised of *Ummul Momineen* Ayesha, the wife of the Prophet, and her cousins Talha and Zubair. Muawiyah led the other group. In the meanwhile, Marwan bin al-Hakam, Usman's secretary, along with some others members of Umayyad clan, managed to escape to Syria to join Muawiyah, carrying Usman's blood-stained shirt and severed fingers of Naila, the caliph's widow. He used it all for propaganda purposes. Soon a severe vilification campaign was launched against Ali. From Syria then came the call for vengeance for Usman's death.

Usman's murder was not a simple assassination committed by an individual to settle personal grievances, as had been the case in Umar's martyrdom. It was a revolt against the then ruling establishment and a fast changing socio-economic milieu. It was not personally against the caliph. [49] Although, Usman had understood the fast changing situation, it was, however, too late for him to take any corrective step.

During the caliphate of Ali (656-661 C.E.), the situation remained confused and perplexing. There were different groups with antagonistic approaches and diverse interests. If one group was satisfied, the other group became violently active. Ali wanted to punish the murderers of Usman but the situation was such that "his entire soldiery numbering 10,000 turned up with lances in their hands crying that all of them were responsible for the murder of Usman. If punishment was to be accorded to any one, all of them should be punished...If the persons demanding the punishment to the murderers of Usman had adopted the right course, they should have extended their support to the Caliph, to enable him to enforce the law. It was then that they should have called for punishing the culprits in keeping with the laws of *shariah*". [50]

Ali took the stand that the people demanding punishment should first submit to the head of the state, then the heirs of Usman should lodge a plaint against the offenders and the law of *shariah* would take its course. "Ali had taken the stand that the authority and prestige of the Caliph must be vindicated. This was exactly the same attitude of Usman during the blockade and his refusal to abdicate. Acquiescence of any caliph to the unreasonable demands of insurgents for fear of difference among the Muslims or a real or imaginary danger would have led to losing the confidence of the people reposed in him". [51] In the course of time, Ammar bin Yasir's assassination made it clear, without doubt, that Ali was right in his stand and those who were pushing for the revenge belonged to rebellious and mutinous group. [52]

Between the family of Umayyad and the family to which the Prophet belonged, the Hashemite, there had been even in the days of paganism, many disagreements and discords.

When the Prophet began his mission, the hostility deepened and intensified. There were violent clashes too. It was only after the conquest of Makkah that the Umayyads accepted Islam. [53] They and other such clans were known as *"tulqa"*. The Prophet granted them a general amnesty. From among them, a few prominent persons were: Abu Sufiyan, Muawiyah, Waleed bin Aqba, Marwan bin Al-Hakam, etc.

Internal Strife

Ali was caliph for a period not more than four and half years. This period of Ali (656-661 C.E.), was marked by civil wars such as Battle of Jamal (36 A.H. /656 C.E.), Battle of Siffin (37 A.H./657 A.H.), Battle of Nahrwan (38 A.H./658 C.E.). In the battle of Jamal, fought near Basra, the number of dead was 10,000. In the battle of Siffin, the death toll was 70,000. Battle of Nahrwan was a battle between Ali and the *Kharijites*. It was fought at Nahrwan, a place twelve miles from Baghdad. The battle took place on the 9th Safar, 38 A.H. It should be noted here that the Battle of Jamal was the first civil war in the Islamic history where Muslims were fighting against Muslims. In all more than 80,000 persons were killed.

Before the Battle of Jamal actually began, for three days, Ali invited his adversaries for a dialogue and compromise. Every day for three days, on behalf of Ali a person raised Quran in his hand and asked them what the battle was for? He was assassinated and like that, three persons from Ali's side were killed. On the fourth day, Ali declared that the battle was unavoidable. [54] At the same time, he was careful enough to instruct his soldiers: "Do not chase when a soldier (after being defeated) is running away; do not kill a wounded soldier; peace and security to those who keep their doors closed; peace and security to those who surrender; their wealth will not be treated as *ghanimah*; women's honour will be protected; children will not be imprisoned". [55]

Yahaya bin Saeed narrates that on the day of battle, Ali issued certain instructions at a time when defence preparedness was on its climax and soldiers were ready to strike at any time. "None should first start shooting and man-slaughtering; speak with them (adversaries) in soft tone. This indeed is the time of reckoning. Whosoever succeeds here, he succeeds on the Day of Judgment. We refrained from attacking. All of a sudden, the adversaries started shouting. Ali asked Muhammad bin Hanifa as to what the cry was? It was told to Ali that they were crying for the revenge of Usman's murder. Ali raised his hands and pointing toward skies prayed: "Oh my Lord! Crush the assassins of Usman". [56] At this particular moment, Ali embraced his eldest son Hasan repeatedly and remarked: "It was better that I was dead twenty years earlier". [57] The words "twenty years" are more touching. A little more than twenty years earlier, the Prophet and his daughter Fatima, wife of Ali, had passed away.

During the course of Battle of Siffin, Ali commented that the dead from both the sides will be surely in the heaven, provided they have fought for the sake of Allah's pleasure. "The real issue (of entering into heaven) will be between me and Muawiyah". [58] The author of *Kanz ul ummal* has reported Ali as saying: "The Prophet of Allah remarked that there will be several dissensions after me. Support Ali if you are there. He is the one who sides with truth against evil". [59]

Malevolent Attitude of *Kharijites*

Abu Ubaid, on the authority of Ibn Abbass, in his classical work *Kitab al Amwal,* has cited an important episode, which throws ample light on the exemplary behaviour of Ali with regard to his detractors, the *Kharijites*. [60] Ibn Abbas reports that he approached *Kharijites* at a place called Haruria to engage them in dialogue and convince them on the futility of a war. The *kharijites* raised three issues. First, Ali accepted arbitration of a third person [61] and accepted his command while the Quran says: "The command rests with none but God" (6:57). Secondly, Ali fought against his detractors and after the war was over he did not imprisoned their men, women and children. He also did not declare their wealth as a *ghanimah* (war booty). It meant that Ali did not considered them all as infidels. He considered them as believers and war was not permissible against believers. Thirdly, Ali had erased the title of *Ameerul Muminum* from his name and, therefore, he ceased to be the commander of faithful.

After listening to the above-mentioned issue, Ibn Abbass said that he himself would provide answers. They *kharijites* agreed. In response to the first issue, Ibn Abbass quoted from Quran: "If ye fear a breach between them twain, appoint (two) arbiters, one from his family and the other from hers; if they wish for peace God will cause their reconciliation; for God hath full knowledge and is acquainted with all things (6:35)". Ibn Abbass impressed upon them that the Almighty Allah Himself has made it clear the necessity of making someone as *hakam*.

Regarding the second issue, Ibn Abbass said how was it possible to imprison Aayesha, a lady who enjoyed the status of mother of *ummah*? It would be against the teachings of Quran if we did not considered her as the mother. It appears in the Quran. "The Prophet is closer to the believers than their own selves; and his wives are their mothers" (33:6). Regarding the third issue, Ibn Abbass reminded them about the pact of Hudaibiya (628 C.E.) when the Prophet himself had asked Ali to erase the title of *Rasullallah*. [62] Just by erasing the title, the Prophet did not cease to be prophet. Similarly, Ali did not cease to be caliph when he erased the title of *ameer ul momineen*.

We can make two important observations. First, all the dead claimed to profess the same faith. In all, more than eighty thousand persons died. Combined together, this number far exceeds the one in all battles fought by Muslims earlier. Secondly, in all these battles Ali did not strike first even though the battles were forced upon him. It is reported by Abu Ubaid on the authority of Abu Majaz that Ali had instructed his commanders not to attack *kharijites,* his bitter opponents, unless they go against the established rule. [63] It happened that the *kharijites* kidnapped Abdullah bin Khubab.

On the way, they saw a few dates falling from the tree. Someone from them picked up a date and started eating. His colleagues abused him arguing that who has allowed him to pick up and eat the date? He threw it out from his mouth. After some time, on the way, another person pricked a pig with his sword. His colleagues scolded him as to who has authorized him to pierce the sword? Abdullah bin Khubab was observing all these. He told them that should not he point out a more sacred thing than a date and a pig?

When allowed, he said that he himself and his life are more sacred. Upon this, the *kharijites* killed him there and then only. When Ali came to know of this, he asked the *kharijites* to pay blood money. *Kharijites* refused maintaining that all of them are murderers of Abdullah bin Khubab. It was then that Ali permitted his men to attack *kharijites*. [64]

Two years later, in 661 C.E./40 A.H., *kharijites* sent out three persons to assassin Ali, Muawiyah and Sa'ad bin Abi Waqas. The latter two survived but Ali was assassinated. Ali fell to sword of a misguided *kharijite* when he had come to the mosque to lead the Morning Prayer. Ibn Kathir has given the following account of the last days of Ali. "The commander of the faithful felt very much disgusted by the prevailing conditions. His army was undisciplined and unruly. The people of Iraq also started defying him and withdrew their cooperation. Syrians on the other hand were gaining strength and making raids on his territories. Ali Ibn Abi Talib was the most virtuous man then living on this earth, the most worshipful, the most selfless, the most learned and the most God-conscious, yet he was forsaken by all...". [65]

Death Before Death

Ali was martyred on Friday 17th of Ramadan 40 A.H./ 24th January 661. Three days later, he breathed his last. At that time, he was 63 years old and was caliph for four years and nine months. Ali is reported to have remarked: "I am not dying today. I died on the day when Usman was assassinated". [66]

In his dying will, Ali advised his sons, Hasan and Husain, saying: "Oh sons of Abul Muttalib, do not shed the blood of Muslims aimlessly and do not kill anybody save my assassin. Listen! If I die by this single stroke, you should also strike him once. Do not mutilate him for I have heard the Prophet forbidding mutilations of any living being after killing it, even if it be a barking dog". [67]

It should be carefully noted here that while assuming the burden of caliphate, Ali was particular about the sanctity of blood of his fellow beings, while dying too he remained particular about it, even of his assassin. In his lifetime, Ali treated human blood as the most sacred.

Nomination

Someone asked Ali on his deathbed whether he would like to appoint someone as his successor, he replied: "No! I leave you as the Prophet had left you". [68] Those attending him insisted for some nomination saying what would be his reply to the Almighty Allah that he left His people without a head? Ali replied: "I would say to Allah that thou appointed me a Caliph when Thou willed and when Thou took me up, I left them to Thy charge. Mend or spoil them as Thou Will". [69]

Ali desperately tried to revive the earlier values, he ultimately died disillusioned, what he wanted to achieve was no longer in keeping with historical facts. An interesting observation is made by al-Daudi in his book *Kitab al-Amwal*: "All the four rightly guided caliphs died and every one of them had worthy sons, who deserved caliphate, had it ever been entrusted to them. But none of them did so out of the fear of Allah and due to compassion for others". [70] Ali's brief reign was full of turmoil. However, Ali, despite great pressure on him, remained uncompromising and fought alone, for principles, until he was assassinated.

Ali led a very simple, unpretentious and unostentatious life and had no personal ambitions. Ali wanted to reinforce Islamic values in both letter and spirit. In place of getting support and cooperation, more number of people started opposing him. "What most tragic was that even his faithful followers like Abdullah bin Abbas whom he had appointed governor of Basra did not obey his strict instructions in respect of the code of conduct and fell prey to the temptation of wealth". [71]

Systemic Failure

By the time Ali became caliph, the conditions had changed so drastically that despite his best possible efforts to restore the early values of Islam and establish a just society, nothing much could be achieved. Ali did his best even though internal troubles did not allow him to concentrate much on economic and financial affairs.

There is no doubt that Ali could not establish his rule over all the occupied territories. It was not his personal failure, but circumstances failed him. At best, it was a case of personal success but collective failure. "Moreover, along with Ali and his caliphate that rebellion also finally failed which as the rebels claimed was started against Usman regime in order to protect the purity, tolerance and justness of the Islamic caliphate and to do away with selfishness waywardness and other evils which had crept in". [72]

In fact, the greatness of Ali was of such dimension that he towered very high above the people around him. It was a case of Gulliver in the lands of dwarfs. He was so high that he could not bend to meet the people and people were so low that they could not rise to meet him. "As such a proper equation could not be established between Ali and the people around him and that was the main cause why he was frequently betrayed and why he did not succeed in the affairs of the world as the ordinary men succeed. He was very much in advance of his age and the people of his age could not keep pace with him". [73] There were many betrayals against Ali, which over the time, weakened his position. Ali lost the game not because he was weak and feeble but because he followed the rules of game with all sincerity and honesty.

End Notes

1. Nadwi, Sayed Abul Hasan Ali, *The Life of Caliph Ali,* op. cit., p. 11.
2. Hanbal, Ahmad bin, *Musnad*, Egypt, 1949, Vol. II, p. 535.
3. *Tarikah ul Khulfa*, p. 224.
4. Siffin located close to the city of Allepo in Syria. The damage done at the battle was great. Muawiyah lost 45,000 men and 25,000 men were killed on the side of Ali.
5. Ibid.
6. Nahrwan, twelve miles from Baghdad.
7. *Nahjul Balagha,* p. 17.
8. Nadvi, S.A.A., *The Life of Caliph Ali,* op. cit., p. 180.
9. Ibid.
10. In some traditions it has appeared as Thursday. Fresh accounts were started on Friday.
11. Actually the translator of *Kitab al Amwal* should have used the word 'yellow'.
12. Al-Daudi, *Kitab al Amwal*, op. cit., p. 117.
13. *Nahjul Balagha:* Letter No. 57, p. 514.
14. Taha Hussain *Al-Fitnat al Kubra,* quoted by Asghar Ali Engineer, *The Origins and Development of Islam,* Ikraq, Kuala Lumpur, 190, p. 124.
15. These episodes are adopted from *Nahjul Balagha*. Reports similar to these are also available in other books which can be conveniently cross-checked.
16. Al-Daudi, *Kitab al Amwal,* op. cit., p. 203.
17. Zayadan, Jurji, *History of Islamic Civilisation: Umayyads and Abbasids*, op. cit., p. 39.
18. *Kanzul Ummal*: Narration No. 14347.
19. *Kanzul Ummal:* Narration No. 36549.
20. One of the two most trusted companions and personal attendants of Ali.
21. *Kanzul Ummal*: Narration No. 31640.
22. This is exactly what Ali had earlier spoken before Usman when complaints against Usman's governors had started multiplying and that there was a open revolt against Usman.
23. In addition to *Nahjul Balagha* similar reports are available from

Al-Bidayah wan Nihayah and *Al Hiyatul.*
24. *Kitab al-Amwal:* Narration No. 669.
25. Gulen, Fethullah M., *The Infinite Light: An Analysis of the Life of Prophet Muhammad,* Adam Publishers and Distributors, New Delhi, 2012.
26. *Kitab al-Amwal:* Narration No. 672, *Kanz ul Ummal:*Narration No. 36543.
27. *Kitab al-Amwal:* Narration No. 673, *Kanz ul Ummal:*Narration No. 36545.
28. For a detail account of Abu Dharr Ghifari one may refer to Abdul Khaliq Madrasi's *Ashab-e-Sufa* (Urdu Edition), Maktab Islamia, Delhi, 2007, pp. 57-78.
29. *Nahjul Balagha*: Sermon No. 133.
30. Baksh, Khuda., *Politics in Islam,* Idarah-i Adabiyat-i Delli, first published in 1920 and reprinted in 1981, p. 32. It is English translation of Von Kremer's *Staadsidee des Islam,* originally published in German.
31. Ibid.
32. *Nahjul Balagha,* Sermon No. 214, p. 390.
33. *Nahjul Balagha,* Letter No. 45, pp. 483-486.
34. A piece of body armour made of metal or leather, covering the chest and sometimes the back.
35. Ibid.
36. *Kanz ul Ummal:* Narration No. 14433.
37. *Kanz ul Ummal:* Narration No. 14431.
38. *Kitab al-Amwal:* Narration No. 565.
39. Ibid.
40. *Kanz ul Umaal:* Narration No. 14280.
41. Nadvi, S.A.A., *The Life of Caliph Ali,* op. cit., p. 135.
42. *Kanz ul Umaal:* Narration No. 14282.
43. Ibid.
44. Nadvi, S.A.A., *The Life of Caliph Ali,* op. cit., p. 136.
45. Nadvi, S.A.A., *The Life of Caliph Ali,* op. cit., p. 137.
46. *Kanz ul Ummal:* Narration No. 14313.
47. *Kanz ul Ummal:* Narration Nos.14369 and 14398.
48. Moududi, S.A.A., *Khilaft wa Malukiat,* op. cit., pp.102-104.
49. For a detailed discussion one may refer *Tarikhul Khulfa*, pp. 240-245.
50. Nadvi, S.A.A., *The Life of Caliph Ali,* op. cit., p. 139.
51. Nadvi, S.A.A., *The Life of Caliph Ali,* op. cit., p. 158.

52. *Kanz ul Ummal:* Narration Nos. 33516 to 33531.
53. Makkah was conquered by the Muslims in January 630 A.D. (20th of Ramadan, 8 A.H.).
54. *Kanz ul Ummal*: Narration No. 31683.
55. *Kanz ul Ummal*: Narration No. 31672. The following narrations also deal with the Battle of Jamal: 31675; 31677; 31677, 31684 and 31685.
56. *Kanz ul Ummal*: Narration No. 31681.
57. *Kanz ul Ummal*: Narration No. 31691.
58. *Kanz ul Ummal*: Narration Nos. 31700 and 31707.
59. *Kanz ul Ummal*: Narration No. 32961.
60. For details about *kharijites* one may refer to *Kanz ul Ummal*: Narration Nos. 31540 to 31593.
61. Please refer to the Battle of Siffin where Ali fought against Muawiyah in (657 C.E.).
62. The most important event of the sixth year of Hijra was the Treaty of Hudaibiya. While the Muslims in general did not comprehend the implications of this apparently humiliating treaty, the Prophet had foreseen its great benefits and the soundness of his strategy.
63. *Kitab al-Amwal:* Narration No. 475.
64. Ibid.
65. Nadvi, S.A.A., *The Life of Caliph Ali,* op. cit., p. 166.
66. *Kanz ul Ummal:* Narration No. 36336.
67. Nadvi, S.A.A., *The Life of Caliph Ali,* op. cit., p. 168.
68. *Tarikhul Khulfa,* p. 71.
69. *Tarikhul Khulfa,* p. 7. S.A.A Nadvi, *The Life of Caliph Ali*, op. cit., p. 191.
70. Al-Daudi, *Kitab al Amwal,* op. cit., p. 117.
71. Engineer, Asghar Ali, *The Origins and Development of Islam,* op. cit., p. 115.
72. Engineer, Asghar Ali, *The Origins and Development of Islam,* op. cit., p. 115.
73. Muhammad Razi and M.H. Syed, *Ali: The Lion of Almighty*, Anmol Publications Pvt. Ltd., New Delhi, 2009, p. 238.

4

Economic Policy Earlier to Ali

Introduction

The major goal of the mission of the Prophet was not only to reform corrupt religious practices but also economic practices. Over a period of twenty three years, the Prophet strived hard to achieve this goal. "We do not find any movement or ideology which has transformed the whole nature of man, his entire being from within and without and his individual as well as his community life. The transformation was such that the human society from mosque to the market, from school to the court and from home to the public field...the entire course of human life was changed". [1] The prophetic mission changed class equilibrium in such a way that poor and downtrodden started receiving their due. In this context, we can understand the significance of the prophetic actions such as: (i) abolition of interest; (ii) regular transfer of funds in favour of poor and needy; and (iii) disapproval of unethical economic and trade practices.

The Policy of Distribution

During the time of the Prophet, the inflow of funds was not huge. Further, this inflow was not regular in nature but mainly occasional. At the same time, the financial requirements of the state were limited and that the aspirations of people too were low. They were not demanding too many services from the government of the time. The situation, however, began to change after the sad demise of the Prophet. The number of conquests increased and the area under Islamic rule expanded rapidly facilitating huge inflow of funds to the state treasury.

From the very beginning of the caliphate, Abu Bakr

divided the state revenue among Muslims, following doubtlessly the example set by the Prophet. Every Muslim received his share. True, in the beginning it was very meagre but went on increasing in the following years. In the first year, to every Muslim fell 10 dirham, in the second year, 20 dirham in annuity (*ata*). Men, women, children and even slaves received a like share. No difference was made between those who accepted Islam before or after the conquest of Makkah. [2]

This policy of equal distribution was changed during the period of Umar (634-644 C.E.). He showed preference to those who had accepted Islam prior to the conquest of Makkah. He placed them first followed by those who embraced Islam after the fall of Makkah. Next was the general Muslim population, which obtained an annuity varying from 300 to 400 dirham. Sucklings, at first, were not given an annuity until weaned when they got 100 dirham each. Later Umar altered this arrangement, allowing to all children the same amount. According to another report, he is said to have allowed to every child two *jaribs* (a certain measure of corn) of wheat, two *kists* of oil, one *kist* of vinegar, per month in addition to annul grant of 100 dirham. [3]

Umar prepared a *"diwan"* (register) in order to record disbursement of public funds. Following huge conquests, the amount of stipends increased as under:

1. The widows of the Prophet received an annuity of 12,000 dirham per year.
2. Veterans who had fought in the battle of Badr received 5,000 per year.
3. *Muhajirun* and *ansar* who had accepted Islam before the battle of Badr but had not taken part in battle received 4,000 dirham per year.
4. Children and dependants of *muhajirun* and *ansar* received 2,000 dirham per year.
5. The inhabitants of Makkah and some others received 800 each.

6. The rest of Muslims received an amount between 200 and 600 dirham annually.

Next to the system of annuity *(ata),* Umar concentrated on the development of an orderly system of civic administration in general and financial administration in particular. The lands in conquered countries were divided into two categories: (a) those whose inhabitants concluded an agreement with the Islamic state and agreed to pay *jiziyah* and land tax *(kharaj)* and, (b) those lands which were conquered by the force of arms passed into the possession of the state and were administered for the common benefit of all Muslims. Such lands were declared as 'crown lands', they could not be disposed of, for the simple reason that they were inalienable. In the conquered countries, therefore, there was not an inch of land, actually owned by Muslims. The whole belonged to all, but to no one in particular.

By declaring land property inalienable, the owners could not realise any money in case of sale and had, therefore, no alternative left but to continue in possession of their lands. This policy saved agriculture from neglect and wreckage and the need for agriculture was great for the maintenance of the troops. The original inhabitants, therefore, devoted themselves to cultivation.

All this is undoubtedly true. But, Umar did not succeed completely in building a just and equitable social order. The march of events overtook him. He appeared to be a worried man. Umar was very strict with the people in the matters of God but he was far stricter as far as his own self was concerned. (He saw) danger for himself from things normally not feared...who inflicts rigorous discipline upon himself hardly any other person would do. It is well known that when there was a great famine in *Amr Ramad* he gave up all comforts and took to hard life and ate very little coarse food, if at all he ate...". [4]

The Gap Between Rich and Poor

On realising the widening gap between rich and poor,

Umar said: "Had I done first what I did later, I would have taken away the wealth from the rich and distributed it among the poor". [5] He, however, could not check the concentration of wealth and concomitant imbalances in the socio-economic structure of the early Islamic society. Since Islam has not, in clear terms, denounced possession of wealth, the companions of the Prophet themselves had gradually amassed huge fortunes. There was nothing wrong because they used rightful means and spent wealth for rightful ends.

In desert areas, there was a total absence of the feudal institutions because there was no question of landed estates to grow. In the oases, people owned land collectively. However, in the conquered provinces of Roman and Sassanid empires, the noble owned landed estates and they made cultivators their serfs. After the conquests, Umar brought a major change and ordered abolition of such a system. He declared cultivators as the owners of lands. In addition to this, he gave lands left behind by the Romans to the native cultivators.

Further, Umar prohibited Muslim officers from acquiring landed property in the conquered lands even by purchases from the natives. The rule remained in operation for quite some time. He also prohibited them from cultivation. Since Umar fixed the daily allowances, he issued instructions to all military officers that they should not cultivate lands. [6] After Umar's demise, Muslim soldiers extensively violated his injunction and started acquiring lands for cultivation. The injunction was ultimately abandoned. [7]

Usman, who succeeded Umar, was a large hearted and soft person. He did not draw any allowance from the treasury for performing the functions of the caliphate. He was a wealthy man and he hardly had any need to draw any allowance from the treasury. He had a different concept of *bayt al maal.* He was of the view that "the amount in the treasury was not the property of the Muslims. After the Muslims had received their due share, all that was there in the public treasury was the property of Allah and not of the Muslims".

As the caliph was in charge of the affairs of the state, he was a trustee of such property and he could utilise funds, on his own authority in public interest, according to his best judgement. He honestly felt that he had the right to utilise the public funds, according to his best judgement and no one had the right to criticize him for that. His argument was that if he could not spend the fund at the disposal of the state at his discretion, then what was the fund in being caliph? [8]

Unscrupulous persons in general and his kinsmen in particular took advantage of his soft nature. [9] "On assuming office, Usman increased stipends by 25 percent". [10] This speaks of heavy inflow of revenue to the then treasury. He could not restrain the rapacity of the governors. The policy of restraining Muslims from acquiring or owning landed property in conquered countries was given up. Muawiyah, the governor of Syria and a cousin of Usman, to whom Umar refused such permission, coaxed the caliph into granting his request. He wrote to Usman that his pay was not sufficient to meet the expenses of the numerous military officers and Greek envoys that were frequently at his court.

He, therefore, begged the caliph to grant ownerless lands, which were considered as 'crown lands' belonging to the entire Muslim community. They were leased out by the state and their rent was paid to treasury. Usman consented the request and precisely in the same manner did Usman act in other provinces. In the caliphate of Umar, when Talha had purchased the estate of Nashtsag, in Kufa, Umar had annulled the transaction. Usman, however, allowed it. Thus, the caliph dealt with the crown lands differently. Earlier, Umar had regarded these lands as the common property.

Usman took another decision of far reaching economic consequences. In order to induce Hejazis settled in Kufa to go back to the Hejaz and to reduce pressure of population on Kufa, he permitted them to exchange their lands held in Iraq with those in Hejaz. Umar had wisely disallowed this. Many took advantage of this opportunity, exchanged their barren lands in Hejaz for the most fertile land in other provinces, and in no time became big holders. Thus, came into existence in an Islamic society a class of big landlords. On the other hand, there was the exploited class that toiled hard.

The very purpose, for which Usman had initiated these measures, i.e., easing the pressure of population in the conquered provinces, remained unfulfilled. The foreign conquests continued and the slaves acquired in the wars continued to pour into these towns. Moreover, in turn, the big landlords and their landholdings created demand for more slave labour. Thus, the measures to ease the pressure population in certain towns, instead of solving the problem aggravated it. It is significant to note that Usman initiated these measures in 30 A.H. and he was assassinated in 35 A.H. Especially, during the last two years of his caliphate, things were moving from bad to worst.

Fadak was a fertile tract near Khaibar under the Jewish occupation, just three miles from Madinah, now the modern village of Howeyat. After the victory of Khaibar, the Prophet sent his envoy, Muhit to Yusha bin Nun, the chief of the village Fadak. The chief of the Jews preferred peace to fighting and surrendered. A peace treaty was concluded between the Prophet and the Jews that they would surrender 50 percent yield of Fadak to the Prophet each year. After passing away of the Prophet, the ownership claims made by Fatima, the Prophet's daughter were rejected and Fadak was declared as the state property.

Usman presented the estate of Fadak to Hakm ibn Abu al-Auss, a kinsman, who under compulsion had accepted Islam and for betraying the Prophet, had been banished to Taif. He likewise sanctioned many important positions to his relatives, the Umayyads. Thus, the *ansar* who in the lifetime of the Prophet and under Umar had received prominence suddenly found themselves superseded. The *ansar* in particular and people in general were not inclined to accept or to submit to the new changes. Usman's gifts to his cousin and to others did not go down well. The *muhajirun* and *ansar,* who had fought the battles; shared the joys and sorrows of the Prophet and with their sacrifices Islam came to be securely established, now had to retire to oblivion and to see the Umayyads were coming to the forefront.

Accumulation of Wealth

Ibn Khaldun gives an account of the wealth accumulated by some of the Prophet's companions. He writes: "In the days of Usman, the men around Prophet Muhammad acquired estates and money. On the day Usman was killed, 1,50,000 dinars and 1,00,000 dirham were in the hands of his treasurer. The value of his estates in Wadi al-Qura and Hunayn and other places was 2,00,000 dinars. He also left 1,000 horses and 1,000 female servants. Talha's income from Iraq was 1,000 dinars a day and his income from the region of ash-Sharh was more than that. The stable of Abd ar Rahman b. Awf contained 1,000 horses.

He also had 1,000 camels and 10,000 sheep. Zayad b. Thabith left silver and gold that was broken into pieces with pickaxes, in addition to the other property and estates he left, in the value of 1,00,000 dinars. Az-Zubayr built for himself a residence in al-Basra and other residences in Egypt, Kufa and Alexandria. Talha built one in al-Kufah and had his residence in Madinah improved. Sa'd b.Abi Waqqas built himself a residence in Madina and has it plastered inside and out. Yala b.Munyah left 50,000 dinars and estates and other things the value of which amounted to 3,00,000 dirham". [11]

After quoting this all from al-Masudi, ibn Khaldun makes an interesting observation. "Amassing worldly property is reprehensible but it did not reflect upon them upon them, because the blame attaches only to waste and lack of planning. Since their expenditure followed a plan and served the truth and its ways, amassing so much property helped them along on the path of truth and served the purpose of attaining the other world". [12]

Since wealth was taxed by the way of *zakah* and income was not taxed, the disparities started widening alarmingly. To top it all, during the period of Usman the collection of *zakah* by the state machinery was stopped. It was done for two reasons. First, there was sufficient money in the state treasury. Secondly, it was not possible to maintain accounts of all the citizens' wealth. [13] The individuals were, therefore, encouraged to pay *zakah* directly to the poor and needy.

Departures in Fiscal Management

In the area of fiscal management, Caliph Usman departed from the practices of his predecessors mainly because of changed financial scenario. It is a well known fact that the first two caliphs had led a very simple and rugged life for themselves and their families because the circumstances so required. Whenever Umar ordered people to do something, he expected his relatives to be the example to the rest of Muslims in following that order. Usman used to say: "It was for the sake of and out of fear of God that Umar used to deny favours to his relatives. I bestow upon my relatives for the sake of God". [14]

On some other occasion, he remarked: "Abu Bakr and Umar, in the context of their policy toward *bayt al maal,* preferred remaining in poverty and they favoured same for their relatives. I, however, favour kind and soft approach". [15] He was correct because huge funds were available with the *bayt al maal.* Even then, there were at least a dozen departures from the early practices. [16] However, in a public address delivered in the Mosque of the Prophet, Usman defended himself and denied all the allegations levelled against him. [17]

During the period of Usman, because of the changes in economic policy many companions of the Prophet grew rich. "Brisk building activity took place in Madinah. Many palatial buildings came up in the city and city expanded a good deal". [18] The Quraish, shrewd businessmen as they were, took full advantage of the liberal policies of Usman. Their trading activities flourished and they amassed huge fortunes. With this wealth they started purchasing lands in conquered territories. "The policies of Usman though conceived in public interest had serious political repercussions. Economic power came to be concentrated in the hands of a small group". [19]

It is wrong to blame Usman for changes in economic policy. "As the caliph was the head of government, he obviously had the authority to disburse funds for such purposes as he thought necessary. A caliph is, however, not an absolute ruler and if there is anything wrong with his exercise of discretion he can certainly be called in question. Thus, while we can hold that the caliph had the right to spend the money on his own authority, it has also to be conceded that the people had the right to criticise the caliph in case had had not exercised his discretion properly". [20]

Times had changed and so also the aspirations of people. Difficulties arose because a few grew rich overnight taking advantage of changes. Gulf between haves and have-nots increased disturbing adversely the class balance. It was not that these developments were noticed at a very later period. These were noticed much early as is clear from the following passage appearing in al-Daudi's *Kitab al-amwal*. "When the people other than the companions of the Prophet took over the administration, the affairs changed a little, till Umar ibn Abd al-Aziz became caliph.

He administered justice, righted wrongs and restored to the owners what the chiefs of Banu Umayyah and others had assigned as *iqta*". [21] The fact that many complaints of forceful possession by strong were brought before Umar bin Adul Aziz shows that the process of acquiring land was not fair in all cases. "Umar bin Abdul Aziz himself declared that more than half of the wealth was in the hands of Banu Marwan and that most of it was acquired through means not permitted by the *shariah*. [22]

The following dialogue between Umar bin Abdul Aziz and

Hisham bin Abdl Malik sheds still more light on undesired developments. "Hisham ibn Abdl Malik entered (in the chamber of) Umar ibn Abdl Aziz. Hisham said: 'You have changed the practice of your own people and altered their decisions and enabled the critics to criticise them'. He (Umar) said: Are you impartial'. He said: Yes. Umar said: By Allah. Hisham said: By Allah. He again said: By Allah. Hisham said: By Allah. He repeated: By Allah. Hisham said: 'By Allah'. Umar then said to Hisham: 'What do you think of a case when a man entrusts his minor children to another person whom he had appointed trustee over them and administrator of their affairs.

The person then usurps their wealth and offers the same as a bequest to his own sons, gets them settled on it, writes for them the deed of ownership therein and makes other persons witnesses to it. Then others grow up and demand their property from them. If you (Hisham) happened to be the judge how would you then decide the case? Hisham said: I will restore it to its owners'. Umar said: The person had already made a deed duly witnessed in favour of his children and long a long time had passed over it'. Hisham said: 'Even then if the case be like this?' Umar ibn Abdl Aziz said: 'By Allah what is the difference between your case and between this?' 'Not even like and he made signs to a little bit of the earth'. [23]

Two Major Developments

Two major developments later created problems during the caliphate of Ali and because of that Ali in particular and other Muslims of the time in general had to suffer heavily. [24] The first one was the continuation of Muawiyah as the governor of Syria and allotment of more areas under his governorship. [25] Secondly, the appointment of Marwan as the secretary did not go down well with the companions of the Prophet in particular and public in general. Marwan in turn exploited the soft nature of Usman to the advantage of his clan. He started acting without informing the Caliph well in advance and more importantly, he spoiled friendly relations between Usman and other companions of the Prophet. Marwan spoilt a reconciliation bid worked out by Ali between Usman and Egyptians. Even Naila, Usman's wife, used to complain against the conduct of Marwan.

The governors of different provinces had also started deviating from the early path. From example, it is reported that Waleed ibn Aqabah took a loan from the treasury of Kufa while he was the governor of city. When the loan matured, the treasurer Abdullah ibn Masud asked him to return it but Waleed did not. When the treasurer demanded the payment, the governor wrote to the caliph complaining about the treasurer. The caliph wrote to the treasurer ordering him to leave Waleed alone with the loan and telling him that he was only the treasurer of the caliph. Upon this Ibn Masud angrily resigned. [26]

A conversation between Caliph Usman and Amr ibn al-Auss who was once the governor of Egypt and replaced by Abdullah ibn Abu Sarh, reveals the mounting pressure on the conquered lands. The caliph said to Amr: "The camels are giving much more milk after you left. (He meant to say that more funds were coming from Egypt after his dismissal). Amr replied: "Yes but their babies have been perished". (He meant that by exacting more taxes from the Egyptians, the Egyptians were impoverished). [27]

The problem is not to judge whether Usman's economic policy was right or wrong and that Usman was weak or strong but to delineate the forces, which had made Usman unable to carry out the ideals of Islam's economic justice. It is argued that it was not due the personal weakness of Usman but there was a "lack of political institutional framework without which ideals and theories are nothing but empty slogans". [28] It is not correct to say that there was a lack of political or administrative framework. It was there and solidly developed during the reign of Caliph Umar. There problem was that the then system was getting weak because of an interplay of several factors.

Pre-Caliphate Economic Vision of Ali

We should study the economic vision of Ali by dividing the discussion into two parts. First, his economic vision before he became the caliph; secondly, his economic policy after assuming the charge of caliphate (656 C.E.). In both periods, Ali had little control over operationalizing his vision. Internal strife greatly marked the period of Ali's caliphate. [29] Ali, therefore, did not get enough time to implement his vision of economic policy.

In Favour of Public Control

During the caliphate of Abu Bakr and Umar, we can visualize the economic vision of Ali through some of his pronouncements. Occasionally, they sought Ali's advice because of his mastery over the knowledge of Quran and traditions of the Prophet. We can cite one such instance from the period of Umar (634-644 C.E.). The Islamic state experienced an extraordinary territorial expansion. Muslims conquered vast areas of Persia, Iraq and Egypt.

When Iraq fell to the Muslim army, the issue of distribution of annexed land came to the fore. The military personnel demanded that the conquered lands should be distributed amongst soldiers only. Their demand was in accordance with the prevailing practice that the benefits of spoils of war should go to the soldiers. Umar called a consultative assembly. Its members Abd al Rahman ibn Auf, Bilal and others were of the opinion that the conquered lands should be distributed among soldiers.

Ali, who was also a member of that assembly, took a different stand. He spoke: "Leave the land to its cultivators as it is so that it becomes a permanent source of economic gain to masses. If land is distributed amongst army personnel it will remain consolidated in some hands forever". [30] Ali suggested that the lands be made a source of income for Muslims and thus be immobilized. [31] If the state distributed lands amongst army personnel only, Ali feared that it would create landlordism in Islam. [32] Yahya bin Adam in his work *Al Kharaj* reports Ali as saying: "O people, guard you souls. Verily if the lands are distributed (a day will come) when seven or nine (landlords) will get hold of village lands. If some of you were not to beat up the faces of others, I would have distributed all of this Sawad among you". [33] Ali was afraid of Muslims becoming overbearing and insolent landlords.

Caliph Umar adopted the same line as that of Ali. He opined that after they had become landlords, the Muslims would start fighting for rights over waters. [34] Umar also found support for his stand in the following Quranic verse. "What God has bestowed on His Apostle (and taken away) from the people of townships, belongs to God, to His Apostle and to kindred and orphans, the needy, the wayfarer; in order that it may not (merely) make a circuit between the wealthy among you"(59:7-8). Accordingly, lands were not distributed amongst army personnel only.

Certain insights clearly emerge, once we observe Ali's stand carefully:

1. Ali was against disturbing the then existing occupancy of cultivators. Any disturbance would have led to several socio-economic repercussions.
2. Continuation of land ownership amongst masses would ensure them a stable source of income.
3. Any displacement would have led to a mass unemployment and loss of income.
4. Mass out migration would have taken place mainly to certain urban centres.
5. At a given point of time, since army members are less in number as compared to masses, transfer of ownership of land from masses to the army personnel exclusively would have led to unequal ownership of resources, more particularly that of land. In other words, Ali was against unequal ownership of resources.
6. As a matter of public policy, Ali held the view that the state should prefer the interest of commoners.

Realizing the gravity of situation Umar argued that "lands may be left under their fire-worshipping owners, and a land tax be imposed on them. And, also *jiziyah* may be collected from them. Out of this income, arrangements may be made to pay salaries to army personnel and fulfil the needs of present and future generations. You tell me yourselves! Will it be possible to retain possession of these regions without a strong border security force to repulse invasions and foreign aggressions?

Shall we not need a strong defence force stationed at different garrison towns to defend the border of the Jazira (Arabia), Kufa, Basra, Iraq, Syria and Egypt? Where are the sources of income? Where from we meet their salaries and allowances and provisions of the people?" This insightful speech of Umar impressed members of consultative committee and they supported him saying: "Yours is the best opinion. How realistic is that what you say and suggest!". [35]

We are now in a position to recognize here that the concern before Umar was the protection of territorial boundaries of the rapidly expanding Islamic state, which involved defence preparedness including salaries to the army personnel. When compared, while Umar's concerns had administrative and security connotations, Ali's concerns had socio-economic undertone. These are not competitive, in the long-run, both are equally important and support each other.

The consultative meeting also suggested the names of Usman bin Hunaif and Hudaifa bin Yaman for the measurement of land and fixing appropriate *kharaj* rates. Usman bin Hunaif was an expert in survey, revenue assessment and accountancy. He enjoyed the post of Settlement Commissioner. [36] When Ali became caliph, he retained the services of Usman bin Hunaif.

End Notes

1. Siddiqui Naeem., *Muhammad: The Benefactor of Humanity*, Markazi Makataba Islamic, Delhi, 6, 1983, p. 1.
2. Khuda Baksh, *Politics in Islam,* op. cit., p. 18.
3. Khuda Baksh., *Politics in Islam,* op. cit., pp. 19-23.

4. Siddiqui M.N., *Islamic Public Economics*, Idarah-I Adbiyat-I Dilli.
5. Siddqui M.N., *Islamic Public Economics*, Idarah-I Adbiyat-I Dilli.
6. Ibid.
7. Engineer, Asghar Ali, *The Islamic State,* op. cit., p. 45. See also Khaliq Ahmad Nizami's *Some Aspects of Religion and Politics in India During The Thirteenth Century,* op. cit., pp. 15-34.
8. Masudul Hassan, *Hadrat Othman Ghani,* Kitab Bhavan, New Delhi, 1999, p. 63.
9. *Kanz ul umaal:* Narration No. 14238. And Khuda Baksh, *Politics in Islam,* op. cit., pp. 28-34.
10. Masudul Hassan, *Hadrat Othman Ghani,* op. cit., on the authority of Raza Misiri, p. 57.
11. *Khaldun Ibn Muqaddimah,* English translation by Franz Rosenthal, Princeton University Press, Princeton, 1970, p. 163. Alo Khaliq Ahmad Nizami's *Some Aspects of Religion and Politics in India During the Thirteenth Century*, op. cit., p. 18.
12. Ibid.
13. Ibid.
14. Moududi, S.A.A., *Khilafat wa Malukiat,* op. cit., p. 83.
15. Ibid.
16. Moududi, S.A.A., *Khilafat wa Malukiat,* op. cit., pp. 90-91.
17. Masudul Hassan, *Hadart Othman Ghani,* on the authority of Raza Misri, op. cit., pp. 184-185.
18. Masudul Hassan, *Hadart Othman Ghani,* op. cit., p. 59.
19. Ibid.
20. Masudul Hassan, *Hadart Othman Ghani,* op. cit., p. 64.
21. Al-Daudi, *Kitab al Kharaj,* op. cit., p. 117.
22. Nizami, Khaliq Ahmad, *Some Aspects of Religion and Politics in India During the Thirteenth Century,* op. cit., p. 19.
23. Ibid.
24. Ibid.
25. Suyuti writes that Muawiyah was governor of Syria for nearly twenty years and for another twenty years he ruled over as the caliph. In all he enjoyed powers for forty years. *Tarikhul Khulfa* p. 288.
26. Al-Baladhuri, *Ansab al Ashraf,* quoted by M.J. Chirri, *The Brother of the Prophet*, op. cit., p. 258.
27. Chirri, M.J., *The Brother of the Prophet*, op. cit., p. 260.

28. Haque, Ziaul, *Landlord and Peasant in Early Islam*, op. cit., p. 234.
29. Three civil wars of far reaching consequences were fought: (i) Battle of Jamal, (ii) Battle of Siffin, and (iii) Battle of Nahrwan. The *kharijites* continued to trouble Ali.
30. *Kitab al-Amwal:* Narrations Nos. 151, 152, 153.
31. Haque, Ziaul, *Landlord and Peasant in Early Islam*, Islamic Research Institute, Islamabad, 1984, p. 191.
32. Haque, Ziaul, *Landlord and Peasant in Early Islam*, op. cit., p. 192.
33. Haque, Ziaul, *Landlord and Peasant in Early Islam*, op. cit., p. 222.
34. *Kitab al-Amwal:* Narration No. 146.
35. *Kitab al-Amwal:* Narration Nos. 146-156.
36. Numani, Shibli, *Al-Farooq*, op. cit., p. 241.

5

Post-Caliphate Economic Policy of Ali

The caliphate of Ali lasted only for four years and nine-months. As pointed out earlier, the internal strife and bloodshed spoiled this short period. Ali, therefore, did not get sufficient time to implement his economic vision to which he gave thought before assuming the charge of caliphate. In this context, Ali's economic policy is studied with reference to: (i) the mobilization, and (ii) distribution of public resources. These two were the prime peacetime concerns of Ali over which he adopted an uncompromising stand. As it will emerge from the following discussion, in several respects, Ali was much ahead of his times.

Mobilization of Resources

Following the huge conquests during the period of Umar, land tax *(kharaj)* became an important source of revenue to the Islamic state so much that it overshadowed significance of *zakah* and *infaq*. The latter two were major sources of transfer of resources in favour of poor and needy during the period of the Prophet and Abu Bakr. It may be recalled here that during the caliphate of Usman, (642-656 C.E.) the state treasury was full. The state gave up direct *zakah* collection; instead, the rich *zakah* payers paid *zakah* directly to the poor and needy.

During the period of Ali, the revenue mobilisation branch consisted of three departments, which separately dealt with three different levies. The land revenue branch handled the collection of *kharaj*; the other two branches managed the collection of *zakah* and *sadaqat* and *jiziyah*. Certain prominent tax initiatives of Ali are discussed as under:

Progressive Taxation of Land

Since time immemorial, land served as a basis of taxation.

Nations and their rulers fought wars mainly for the purpose of territorial expansion so that more land can be brought under the tax net. The Prophet and his rightly guided caliphs too fought wars but the prime concern was either defence or propagation of the faith. Territorial expansion was secondary to the faith. The Prophet changed the very perception of war.

The place from where the Prophet started his mission was desert and hence land taxation was not a prominent issue. In a few areas, people took up agriculture as their occupation. Different agricultural crops, and not the agricultural holdings, came in the *zakah* net. *Zakah* on crops was known as *ushr.* It was collected at the rate of 10 percent or 5 percent depending upon the type of irrigation. It was during the caliphate of Umar that huge land areas, that too very fertile land, came under Muslim occupation. This, consequently, led to the birth of *kharaj.*

Kharaj was a levy on land and it was collected in silver and or gold. Mainly, the centre appointed *Kharaj* officers. The provincial governors were also authorised to appoint *kharaj* officers themselves. Provincial governments retained revenue from *kharaj* and *jiziyah.* As against this, *zakah* and *sadqat* were collected mainly in-kind and their collection was transferred to the centre. During the regime of Umar, Usman bin Hunaif had fixed the following rates:

Table 5.1: Kharaj Rates per Annum for Every Jareeb of Land Planted With

Crop	Rate in Dirhams
Vine	10
Vegetables	12
Sesame	8
Palm trees	8
Sugar beet	6
Cotton	5
Wheat	4
Olive	3
Barely	2

Source: Abu Ubaid, p. 103.

While it is difficult to say what might have made Usman bin Hunaif to determine such rates, it can be said that rates were kept low for two important items namely wheat and barley. Umar inquired from his revenue officers whether the tax rates were reasonable or not? He was much satisfied on being informed that these are reasonable. Usman bin Hunaif further added: "Even if I double the amount I am sure they would afford to pay". Hudaifa said: "What I have spared for them is too much". [1]

Land taxation continued to remain an important issue in Ali's reign too. Ali retained the services of Usman bin Hunaif as his chief treasury officer. Ali, however, made certain changes with regard to the categories of land and *kharaj* rates that reflected his economic insight. The following rates were fixed for per *jareeb* of land. [2]

Table 5.2: Rates per Jareeb of Land

S.No.	Type of crop/land	Rate
1.	Most fertile land (Grade I)	1.5 dirham
2.	Less fertile land (Grade II)	1 dirham
3.	Less fertile land (Grade III)	0.5 dirham

Source: *Nahjul Balagha,* p. 74.

When Table 5.2 is analyzed carefully, it is eminently clear that Ali, in the area of land taxation, introduced an element of progression: the rate of *kharaj* increasing from 0.5 dirham to 1.5 dirham, depending upon the type of land. When we consider land as a taxable asset, the fiscal message of Ali is that even productive assets (*a la* wealth) can be taxed at progressive rates and different slabs can be introduced. Currently, in almost all the countries, wealth is taxed at a proportional rate and that too at a very low rate. The exemption level is kept quite high, consequently many eligible wealth taxpayers remain outside the tax net. Wealth tax, therefore, in relation to income tax, corporation tax and sales tax, occupies a secondary place. This also makes the burden of resource mobilization to fall on income and transactions.

It is also clear from Ali's land tax policy that the tax rate in case of specific crops could be high when their yield/return is high. For example, as compared to a levy of 1.5 dirham on most fertile land (Grade I), he collected 10 dirham (nearly seven-eight times more) from the farmers cultivating vine and palm groves. These crops enjoyed high commercial value. Ali's practice, if adopted and extended to other productive and remunerative assets, will lead to major changes in the taxation of wealth.

Progressive Taxation of Personal Wealth

The *shariah*-based levies are collected at proportional rates. *Zakah* rate, by default, is 2.5 percent on gold, silver and merchandise. We cannot increase or decrease it, whatever might be the situation. Similarly, *zakah* on agricultural produce, known as *ushr*, is collected at the rate of 5 percent or 10 percent, depending upon the type of irrigation. The mineral wealth is taxed at the rate of 20 percent. It is, thus, clear that *zakah* rates, except *zakah* on livestock, are proportional. The interesting point to note is that while individual levies are proportional, the system appears to be progressive, the rates gradually increasing from 2.5 percent to 5 percent, then to 10 percent and finally to 20 percent. The implicit message of *shariah* is that the rate of a tax should not fall below 2.5 percent and should not exceed 20 percent. In a strict Lafferian sense, the highest *zakah rate* as suggested by the shariah does not generate any adverse economic effect.

The contribution of Ali is that he introduced specific progression, be the tax on lands, crops and persons. For example, during his caliphate, Ali classified the non-Muslims protectorates *(ahlul z-zimmah)*, for the purpose of *jiziyah* collection.

Thus, an element of progression was introduced in the administration of *jiziyah* whose basis of charge was possession of wealth. At present, the progressive taxation of wealth is surely a matter of serious consideration. Currently, both at the personal and corporate levels, wealth is not taxed at progressive rate. As pointed out earlier, this makes the burden of tax to fall on income and transactions. More importantly, inequalities get accentuated because these are caused by unequal distribution of wealth. There is much to learn from Ali's tax treatment of *ahlul z-zimmah.* Ali's approach, in case of secular levies, provides much need flexibility particularly at a time when anti-cyclical tax policy is required.

Table 5.3: Classification of Ahlul Z-Zimmah for the Purpose of Jiziyah

S.N	Category	Amount
1	General public	12 dirham per head
2	Businessmen	42 dirham per head
3	Middle class	42 dirham per head
4	Very rich persons and landlords	48 dirham per head

Source: *Nahjul Balagha,* p. 75.

Supply Side Tax Policy

In the matters of taxation, the overall approach of Ali contained "supply side" ideas. This policy attaches importance to the production and productive agents. As against this, the demand management approach attaches importance to regulating/deregulating demand to control economic fluctuations. In the supply side approach 'human incentive', 'factor responsiveness' and 'factor productivity' come to the centre stage. While designing the tax policy of his government, Ali has taken a due note of all these aspects.

In one of the letters written to Malik al-Ashtar, Ali speaks vividly about the factor productivity, in this case the fertility of land: "So far as collection of land revenue is concerned you must always keep in view the welfare of taxpayers which is of primary importance than the taxes themselves. Since actual taxable capacity of people rests on the fertility of land, therefore, more attention should be paid to the fertility of land

and prosperity of the subjects than to the collection of revenue". [3]

Having realised the importance of factor productivity, Ali repeats again the same instruction at another place. "More importance should be attached to the fertility of land than to the collection of taxes because actual taxable capacity of people rests upon the fertility of the land. The ruler who does not pay attention to the prosperity of his subjects and fertility of land but concentrates only the collection of revenue, wastes the land, ruins the state and brings destruction to the creatures of God. His rule cannot last for long". [4]

The above-mentioned instructions of Ali are the golden maxims of taxation that attach importance to the tax base and its attributes and not to the tax rate and amount of revenue collected. This essentially is the message of modern fiscal theorists and public finance experts. [5] Across the globe, tax reforms movements on one hand and tax administrators on the other, have now realized that the tax base is more important than the tax rate. When the base is broad and productive, the government collects more tax revenue with low rates. A regime of high tax rates neither brings in more revenue nor improves the prosperity levels. On the contrary, the efficiency costs of a regime of high tax rates are huge.

Ali is perfectly right when he remarks that a ruler, who is interested only in revenue collection and ignores issues such as fertility of soil and welfare of its people, brings nothing but disaster. People get frustrated when they note that huge sums are collected but efficient administration is missing. They revolt against unjust and corrupt system, sometimes peacefully through ballot boxes and at other times violently. [6]

Minimum Tax Burden

Ali also speaks of 'heavy burden of taxation', and asks his officers to reduce taxpayers' burden as and when the situation warrants, clearly introducing an element of flexibility. In this connection, Ali writes to Malik Ashtar: "If taxpayers complain to you about heavy incidence of taxation, of any accidental calamity, of vagaries of monsoon, of scarcity and stoppage of the means of irrigation, of floods or destruction of their crops on account of excessive rainfall and if their complaints are true then reduce their taxes. This reduction should be such that it provides them opportunities to improve their conditions and eases their circumstances". [7] Here, Ali is speaking of not a nominal or token reduction in tax burden but a realistic one.

Ali also anticipates that on account of reduced taxes, revenue may fall and the state may face financial difficulties. It is very likely that the difficulties may further compound when the state is required to make huge public expenditure to solve economic and social difficulties of its subjects. This is notwithstanding the huge expenditure on internal law and order and defence preparedness. Such a situation may depress any ruler. Ali, however, has a different view when he writes: "Decrease in state income due to such reasons should not depress you, because the best investment for a ruler is to help his subjects at the time of their difficulties.

They are the real wealth of a country and any investment on them even in the form of reduction of taxes, will be returned to the state in the shape of the prosperities of its cities and improvement of the country at large, at the same time you will be in a position to command and secure their love, respect and praise along with the revenues. Will not that be a lasting happiness? Remember Malik! If a country is prosperous and if its people are well-to-do than it will happily and willingly bear any burden". [8]

In the instructions cited above, Ali is clearly speaking about the benefits originating from a just tax policy. In the opinion of Ali, best investment is the one, which is for the sake of human development. This brings "human beings" to the centre stage of development policy. Ali correlates humane approach of the tax policy with the prosperity of cities and their peoples. A just tax policy, as Ali opines, not only nets more revenue but it earns respect and command of the people.

In a prosperous country where there is a 'just' tax system, people will voluntarily come forward to clear their tax dues. Ali tried to incorporate 'human element' into tax administration when, elsewhere, taxes were known as notorious means of exploitation and subjugation.

Yahya ibn Adam quotes Ali as saying: "We are commanded to realize the tax from what is in excess to the needs of the cultivators". [9] Implicitly, here is a golden maxim of taxation: "For tax purpose, ignore the subsistence component of income and tax only the surplus over and above". The subsistence component of income derives its support from Engle's law of consumption.

Conventionally, the payment of taxes, etc., is taken as *quid pro quo*. Payment of taxes is a duty but the taxpayers are asked not to claim anything in return. Ali, however, tagged payment of taxes to the benefits received. A government, which does not provide benefits to its people, in the opinion of Ali, has no moral right to ask for tax payments. In Ali's vision, there is no question of payment when taxpayers do not receive any benefit. This also clears Ali's perception of governance. In this connection, we should note the following narration.

Abu Ubaid on the authority of Ibn Jarih has reported an interesting episode. Once, a person approached Ali with his *zakah* dues. Ali asked him: "Do you receive any stipend or monetary assistance from *bayt al maal*". He replied in negative. Ali then asked him to go back maintaining that the government will not collect anything from him. "We do not want to overburden you. We do not want to trouble you. The first trouble is that you are not paid anything from *bayt al maal.* Secondly, we should not trouble you by imposing *zakah*". [10]

The above-narration also helps us to know that in Ali's views there is a fine convergence of 'benefit and ability to pay principles of taxation'. Ali asks his tax officers to consider the taxable capacity of individuals. This signifies the ability principle. At the same time, he emphasizes that benefits should accrue to the taxpayers. This clearly highlights the benefit principle.

Humane Tax Administration

Ali knew it very well that the governments elsewhere were unpopular among their peoples mainly because of the force used in the matters of tax collection. Tax collectors were a most feared lot. People used to say: "You can have a Lord. You can have a king. The man to fear most is the tax collector". Government machinery ruthlessly collected taxes and callously spent tax revenue.

Ali was always careful about tax collection. He relates the abject and wretched living of people to the desire of rulers and officers to amass huge wealth and possessions using mainly the foul means. They were mainly interested in accumulating huge wealth in the shortest possible time at their disposal. "They never learnt any lesson from the history of nations and never paid any attention to the orders of God". [11]

In this context, Ali's instructions are worth studying from which the humane face of his tax administration emerges. Ali issues detailed instructions to the *kharaj* collectors posted at Ukhana (Baltic region) and also at several other places. They should not lay their hands on the cultivators' clothes, both summer and winter, or articles of their daily sustenance or cattle used in the cultivation or their household objects. They should not sell horses of taxpayers nor their oxen or cows. Ali insisted that they should be kind and lenient in giving taxpayers some convenience to clear their dues.

According to Yahya, a man from Thaqif reports: "Ali b. Abi Talib appointed me to supervise Buzura Sabur (Iranian region) and advised me not to flog any one or sell his provisions, his winter or summer garments, nor the beasts he works with and never to let a man stand (in the sun) while collecting dirham (in taxes). So I said: 'O Commander of Faithful! Then I shall return to you as I left you'. And he replied: '(No problem) even if you return as you left! Beware! We are ordered to collect from them with kindness". [12]

Abu Ubaid, in his classical work *Kitab al Amwal,* narrates that once Ali appointed a person as the *kharaj* collector of Abkari (Yemen) region. While sitting on the pulpit, Ali instructed him to collect *kharaj* diligently, not leaving a single penny. He asked the *kharaj* collector to meet him once again in the afternoon. There upon, Ali said: "I add the following to what I instructed you earlier. You will be dismissed from services if you disobey me. Look! Do not force *kharaj* payers to sell their animals and seasonal clothing to clear their dues. Treat them leniently and as far as possible consider their convenience to clear kharaj". [13] Here also, Ali is asking his tax officers to desist from using force. They should treat taxpayers, who are also human beings, compassionately and as far as possible consider their convenience. Convenience, as we know, is one of the famous canons of taxation. [14]

Once Ali was passing through Ambaz with his army. The rich men of the province, as was the custom of those times, came out to greet him. They offered the best Persian horses as presents and requested his permission to act as hosts to his army. He met them very courteously but very politely refused to accept the gifts and the invitation saying: "You have paid your taxes, to receive anything more from you, even when you offer it voluntarily and willingly, is a crime against the state". When the request was pressed repeatedly, Ali ordered that the horses could be accepted against their taxes and as far as the feast was concerned, it must be paid out of war expenses.

In one of the letters, Ali issued certain guidelines pertaining to the approach of tax officers. Ali asks them to behave cordially. They should maintain their dignity and that their approach should not irritate taxpayers. Otherwise, Ali fears that the entire process of *zakah* collection will become hateful. Ali writes: "Do not give up fearing Allah who has no partner. Do not let the Muslim grieve (over their lot of having you as their ruler) and do not approach them in a way as to make your approach hateful to them. Do not tax them more than what is actually due from them to Allah. When you reach a group of people (tribe or village) to assess a tax on them, then stay only at their watering place (a well or water hole the most convenient place for stay in desert regions) and do not stay in their houses. Then go to them maintaining your dignity and prestige and when you are in their midst, wish them peace and blessings of Allah and show due respect to them. Tell them that the Caliph of Allah has sent you to collect from them their dues to Allah. Ask them whether they possess enough means to pay the dues of Allah that you may gather them and pass them on to His Caliph. If somebody tells you that he does not possess enough wealth to make him liable to pay taxes then do not worry him and accept his plea". [15]

In case if eligible *zakah*payers are found, Ali writes: "If someone tells you that he is in a position to pay *zakah*, then go with him to his house, field or pasture but do not frighten him or make him nervous and do not behave with him with undue harshness or tyranny. Then accept the gold or silver which he offers. If he has cows, bulls, goats and camels then do not enter the herd without his permission because most of it belongs to him (it is not part of *zakah*). If you have to enter the herd then do not enter like the one who is coming there to take possession of the cattle. Do not tyrannize the owner; do not frighten the cattle to make them disperse". [16]

We have noted at several places that, in the collection of taxes, Ali was against the use of force. Here in this letter Ali reiterates his earlier plea. "Do not force anybody to forsake his requirements and to do without his necessities (so that he may pay the taxes). In collection of taxes and revenues, do not sell their winter and summer clothing, their slaves or such of their animals as are of service to them, do not resort to whipping, do not touch their property, be they Muslims or non-Muslims...Be kind to the people, treat the army well and do not hesitate doing your best in helping the subjects and in guarding the religion". [17]

Method of Computation and Assessment

Ali has given detailed instructions regarding the collection of different levies. People used to approach him in the matters of computation of *zakah* and *kharaj* levies. In respect of *zakah* on gold, silver and articles of trade, there were neither slabs nor gradation. *Zakah* was collected at a flat rate. *Zakah* on agricultural produce was collected at the rate of 5 percent or 10 percent, depending upon the method of irrigation.

It was in respect of animal wealth that there were slabs and different rates were applied. Since it was a little complicated, Ali therefore, thought it better to give detailed instructions to his officers. "Then divide the herd into two parts and allow the owner to select the one for himself. If he selects one part for keeping himself, then do not object to it. Again divide the part which he has left for the share of *zakah* to be selected from out of these two parts, again allow him to select the lot that he wants to retain for himself. Never object to his selection. Continue like that until you arrive at the lot that constitutes the share of Allah (*zakah*) then take possession of it.

Even if, in spite of all these precautions, he thinks the division was unfair and unjust, then mix the whole lot and go through the process once again as I have already explained to you till you arrive at the share of Allah *(zakah)* to the satisfaction of everybody concerned. Remember you do not have to accept old and unhealthy camels or such as have their limbs damaged". [18] The overall result of such an assessment was that the "best of livestock" was left with *zakah*payers making them to feel happy. This improved voluntary compliance and *zakah*payers started cooperating with *zakah* collectors.

Transfer of *Zakah* Collection

The next issue addressed by Ali is the safety of livestock and their safe transportation to the seat of caliphate. Here Ali writes: "I want to instruct you once again that you should not entrust these goods and animals to the one who is not honest. Entrust them to one who is trustworthy and who is of a kind and sympathetic disposition. He should not treat the animals cruelly and should not starve them or tire them out during the transit. Instruct him not to separate a she-camel from its young, not to milk it so much that nothing is left for its young one and not to ride them harshly or to overburden them with heavy loads. He should ride them in turns so that those, which are already used, may have an easy journey.

He should not drive them fast and should avoid harshness. He should always give them enough rest at watering places. They should not be driven through deserts. As far as possible, green lands and well-wooded regions should be selected for the passage. Thus, every care should be taken so that they reach their destination in healthy and robust condition without having received any harsh and brutal treatment on the way so that I may distribute them according to the Orders of Allah and the Holy Prophet. Verily, the collection of the dues of Allah in the way that I have explained to you is a pious deed and a religious duty, which will carry its reward before the Lord". [19]

No Room for Misappropriation

Ali then starts dealing with the issue of misappropriation of *zakah* collection. [20] "Be it known to you that the person who misappropriates *zakah* funds, who will fill his stomach with such amounts, and who harms his religion and injures his conscience with such deeds will be punished and disgraced in this world as well as the next. The worst form of dishonesty is the breach of trust of the public funds (*zakah*) and the most despicable example of maladministration is that the Imam should tolerate such forms of dishonesty". [21] Here, Ali is holding both the caliph and his governors responsible for deceit and dishonesty.

From time to time Ali kept issuing directions to his tax-officers who were also responsible for the administration of different provinces. For example, Ali wrote a letter to Muhammad, son of Abu Bakr, the first caliph, when the latter was appointed as the governor of Egypt. "Be fair, just and impartial in your dealings so that influential persons do not dare to take undue advantage of your leniency and less influential and poor may not be disappointed in your justice and fair dealings". [22]

In another letter to the collectors of taxes and revenues, Ali writes as under: "A letter from the creature of Allah, Ali bin Abi Talib, to the collectors of taxes and revenues. One, who does not care for his salvation, will never think of providing for his life after death with good deeds and, therefore, he will not be able to escape the punishment. Be it known to you that the responsibilities laid down upon you are a few but the Divine reward reserved for you is very high. Allah has forbidden you from tyranny and injustice; and even if there had not been any fear of punishment for these inequities, the mere reward of being just, kind and human would have been such that there could not have been any excuse for not trying to achieve it. Treat the taxpayers with equity and justice and think over their wishes with patience and kindness because you are the treasurer of the subjects, representative of the people and the officer on behalf of higher authority. [23]

Salient Aspects

An analysis of above-mentioned instructions brings home certain points:

1. The tax collectors were asked to develop close rapport with taxpayers and win over their confidence.
2. They were prohibited from frightening, threatening, pressurizing or oppressing the taxpayers.
3. It was decreed that the first assessment should not necessarily be the last one. In case of any dispute, there should be reassessment.
4. *Zakah* collectors should not approach *zakah*payers in a way as to make their approach hateful.
5. They should stay only at the watering places and should not stay in *zakah*payers' houses.
6. While approaching, the officers should maintain dignity

and show due respect to *zakah*payers.

7. *Zakah*payers should be informed that the caliph has sent them to collect from them the dues of Allah.
8. If somebody maintains that he hasn't sufficient wealth, then the officers should not trouble him and accept his plea.
9. If someone admits that he has wealth, the officers should follow him to his house, field or pasture. They should not frighten him or make him nervous.
10. Payment, if any, made in gold or silver should be accepted.
11. In case of livestock, officers should not enter into the herd without the permission of owner. Ali instructed them to treat livestock with utmost care.
12. The herd should be divided into two parts and the owner should be allowed to select one for himself.
13. The process of division should continue until the officers arrive at the lot, which constitutes the dues of Allah.
14. The tax officers should not separate she-camel from its young and the officers should not milk it so much that nothing is left for its young-ones.
15. Tax officials should not ride over animals harshly or over burden them with heavy loads. They should allow sufficient rest to animals at watering places.
16. Ali strictly warned tax officers against misappropriation of funds.
17. He instructed them to avoid, as far as possible, the use of force.
18. The very purpose behind all these instructions, according to Ali, was that the tax officers should collect and distribute Allah's dues according to the orders of the Prophet.

From instructions enumerated above it is clear that Ali wanted that his officers should adopt a very humane approach. Ali knew it well that in the neighbouring countries the tax collecting machinery used to harass heavily the taxpayers. People viewed taxation as an instrument of exploitation.

Consequently, there seldom existed cordial relations between taxpayers and the tax collectors. While the former used to avoid taxpayers in order to conceal their assets and evade taxes, the latter used all possible forms of force to collect taxes. We should note that the comprehensive humane approach of Ali was not limited to men alone, even the herds of animals were asked to be treated softly. It is now left to one's imagination to comprehend that when Ali's was so soft towards animals, what would have been his approach towards human beings!

It is argued here that while the above-mentioned instructions are mainly administrative in nature, the following instructions issued to another officer are characterized by a very heavy dose of religiosity. The fear of God and accountability on the Day of Judgment dominate the contents of his instructions. [24] He writes: "I order to keep fear of God in your mind in all such affairs and on all such occasions where there is no one to witness your actions. I order you not to meet Muslims as a tyrant and slanderer, not to ill-treat them, not to calumniate them, because they are your brothers in religion, (they) will help in collecting dues and find means and ways to help poor. Otherwise, there will be many who will complain and protest against you on the Day of Judgment. Woe be to the person against whom poor destitute, beggars and those who have been debarred from their rights of receiving *zakah* complain before the God...(One) who misappropriates *zakah* funds will be punished and disgraced in this world as well as in the next". [25]

In the entire process of collection and distribution of *zakah* funds, Ali holds both the officers, at the lower level, and caliph himself at the higher level, responsible for any lapse. He remarks: "The worst form of dishonesty is the breach of trust of public funds and the most despicable example of mal-administration is that the *imam* (caliph) should tolerate such forms of dishonesty". [26]

Distribution Policy

Economists are of the opinion that the issue of distribution is more difficult to handle. "Yet distribution issues are a major (frequently *the* major) point of controversy in the budget debate. In particular they play a key role in determining tax and transfer policies". [27] In the absence of any clear policy of distribution, factor endowment and factor pricing determine the distribution of income. The distribution, in the absence of government intervention, may not be necessarily fair or just. It may not correspond to certain societal values. Most would agree that some adjustments are required to prevent the distribution from a further deterioration.

The call for redistribution is based upon social philosophy and value judgments that are normally difficult to translate into action. Yet, the dominant consideration is that the redistributive policies should lead to the maximization of total happiness. Among the various fiscal devices, direct taxes and transfer-payments, particularly the transfer of cash, mainly cause the redistribution.

Early Contours of Distribution

The economy of early Islamic state was quite rudimentary in character. Hence, there was no sophisticated allocation of resources. It is, however, to the credit of Islam that it rearranged the distributive role of the government budget wherein the financing of requirements of poor and destitute received top priority. In the history of the world religions, before the Prophet, none ever made an institutionalized effort to restructure the economic position of poor and destitute through the state intervention.

During the period of Prophet, the contours of distribution policy had started emerging. In the beginning, the Prophet provided financial assistance to needy and poor on an *adhoc* basis. When revenue started multiplying, the Prophet regularized the whole process of distribution. Two principles decided the sharing of resources. [28] First, every fighter was paid according to his *efforts*; foot soldier was paid one share and horseman was given two shares, one for himself and the other for his horse. Secondly, everyone was paid according to his *needs*, a bachelor was paid one share and a married person was paid two shares. The first principle took care of human incentive, the second principle, aimed at satisfying personal requirements of a family.

The first caliph, Abu Bakr (632-634 C.E.) also followed same policy. Umar and other companions of the Prophet argued for a change in the policy asking Abu Bakr to adopt a policy of preference to which he politely refused. He maintained that in the matters of livelihood a policy of equality is better than a policy of preference. Al-Daudi reports: "Abu Bakr used to make equal distribution among people saying: 'Those who preceded in accepting Islam by their activities, were sure to get their reward from Allah, but this property was only a means of living in which people were equal. Ali did so. Umar and Usman used to give on the principle of priority". [29]

After the demise of Abu Bakr, Umar became the caliph (634-644 C.E.). He replaced the policy of equal distribution by a policy of preference. However, Umar, later on realizing the emerging disparities, decided to change the policy that he was following since seven years, from 16 A.H. to 23 A.H. He swore that that if he lived next year, he would equalize distribution of grants. Ibn Saad reported: "I heard Umar bin Khattab saying: 'I swear by Allah. If I happen to remain alive next year on this occasion, I would join (the names of persons appearing at the end in the *fai* register with those) names appearing at the beginning and make them one' (i.e., equal in getting their share of *fai*). [30] His martyrdom, however, prevented him from realizing the stated goal.

The implications of unequal distribution were more eminent during the caliphate of Usman bin Affan (644-656 C.E.). He was by nature very generous. At personal level, he led a simple life but was very open-handed in awarding others.

Some members of his clan took undue advantage in securing plump positions in the government, which they utilized to serve their own ends. [31] "State allowances increased during the time Usman so much so that a slave girl was bought according to her weight, a horse for twenty thousand dirham and a palm tree for one thousand dirham". [32]

Ali's policy of abstinence and detachment, did not allow him to see the inequalities growing. At the public level, his impartial stand, did not allow anyone, including his brothers, relatives and officers to lead a life of extravagance at the cost of mass poverty. After assuming, the mantle of caliphate in his very first address Ali said: "Listen! Whosoever amongst the companions of the Prophet holds the view that because of his companionship (with the Prophet) he has superiority over the others should know that this superiority will benefit him tomorrow before God who will reward him for it. In fact, you are all servants of God and this wealth is God's. It will be distributed equally among you. In this respect no one has preference over others; however, God has the best reward for God fearing". [33]

Policy of Equal Distribution [34]

When Ali became caliph, he changed the policy of unequal distribution. At this juncture, it is interesting to recall here an earlier event. During the time of the Prophet, Ali was deputed to Yemen. Thereat, he followed the policy of equal distribution of funds and spoils of the war. This made a few companions to complaint against him to the Prophet when he was returning from his Farewell Pilgrimage (632 C.E.). By the orders of the Prophet, his companions erected a special platform. After the afternoon prayers, the Prophet sat on the pulpit and made his last public address. Taking Ali's hand, the Prophet asked his followers whether he was not superior in authority and person *(awla)* to the believers themselves. The crowd cried out in one voice: "It is so, O Apostle of God". He then declared: "Of whom I am the *mawla* [the patron, master, leader, friend], of him Ali is also the *mawla [man kuntu mawlahu fa Ali-un mawlahu]...".* [35] The resentment of a few against Ali was because of his policy of distribution. By declaring Ali as the *mawla,* the Prophet endorsed the distribution policy of Ali.

When Ali took the charge of caliphate, he found that large fiefs and estates were granted to certain persons. A few well-wishers advised Ali to overlook and ignore previous distribution. He, however, handed back all the fiefs and estates to the public treasury. On that occasion, he remarked: "By God! If I had found that public money had been squandered in celebrating marriages and in purchasing slave-girls, I would have taken them back and would have handed them over to the country because functions and responsibilities of justice and equity are far-reaching and far-extending. One, who does not boldly act according to the dictates of justice and fair-play, will feel very nervous in facing tyranny and oppression". [36]

Impartiality and equity were hallmarks of Ali's policy of distribution. This was a subject very dear to Ali. In return, this policy caused him to lose many supporters and followers. This is eminently clear from a lengthy conversation, over the policy of distribution, between Ali and Usman bin Hunaif, his chief Treasury Officer. The latter told him that: (a) by introducing the principle of equal distribution of wealth; (b) bringing important persons down to the level of commoners; (c) by raising the status of Negros and Persians to that of Arabs; (d) by allotting shares to slaves equal to their masters; (e) by depriving rich persons of their entitlements, and (f) by stopping special grants to them according to their status, Ali had done more harm to himself and his cause than good.

Continuing this he further said: "Look my Lord! These are the reasons why influential and rich Arabs are deserting you and are gathering around Muawiyah. Of what use these poor persons, disabled people, aged widows and Negro slaves are to you? After listening to Usman bin Hunaif carefully, with deep anguish Ali replied: "I cannot allow rich and influential persons to exploit the society of this Muslim state and to run an inequitable and unjust system of distribution of wealth and opportunities. I cannot for a moment tolerate this. This is a public wealth; it comes from the masses it must go back to them.

The rich and powerful persons have not created any wealth, they have merely sucked it from masses and after paying the taxes what is left to them is many times more than what they pay to the state and they are welcome to retain it. Had all this been my private property, I would have gladly distributed it in the same manner. As far as their desertion is concerned, I am glad that they have deserted me. As far as the usefulness of services of these disabled persons and have-nots is concerned, remember that I am not helping them to secure their services; I fully know they are unable to serve me. I help them because they cannot help themselves and they are as much human beings as you and I. May God help me to do my duty as He wishes me to do". [37]

From the first reading, it appears that Ali had taken an extreme stand. It is, however, incorrect. He allowed the rich to retain the post tax wealth. He has also made it clear that his policy of equal distribution is free from any motive and sans *quid pro quo*. It is not in exchange of their services. He admits that the poor are so poor and helpless that they cannot help Ali in his fight against socio-economic inequalities. He admits that they are unable to serve him because they are too poor to help themselves. For them there is no escape from the trap unless the government extends its helping hand.

It further appears in *Nahjul Balagha* that several delegations headed by Zubair, Ibn Abbas, Ibn Hunaif, etc., met Ali and asked him to have a relook at the whole policy of distribution. On each occasion, Ali explained to them the principles of equity and justice. He maintained: "Do you want to seek help by oppressing and tyrannizing the people over whom I am appointed by the God to rule. By God, this will not happen…I can never abuse the power rested in me nor can I be cruel towards human beings.

Had it all been even my personal property I would have distributed equally amongst the needy and poor...Beware! that to spend upon undeserving occasions and to give to undeserving persons is a dissipation and a waste of wealth...Unjustifiable and undeserving donations may enhance the status of a man among his worldly surroundings but he is sadly humiliated in the eyes of God...these undeserving beneficiaries usually turn against him in the times of distress and he finds them as his worst enemies censuring his actions and blaming him for his lavish grants". [38]

Ali's own brother, Aqeel, was suffering from extreme poverty. He requested Ali to spare (about five kilograms of) wheat from public granary. Starvation had turned his children into living skeletons and had changed their colour to blue. Aqeel was relentless in his demand to procure something out of turn from the public granary. Thereupon, Ali asked someone to take Aqeel to the market and asked Aqeel to break open a few shops and take away whatever he wanted. Amused, Aqeel asked Ali: "Do you want that I should steal from the shops and then get arrested? Ali replied: "Do you want that I should steal from the *bayt al maal* to favour you? [39]

There is another narration to the effect that Aqeel was indebted. He sought some money from *bayt al maal* to clear his debts. Ali refused to oblige him. Upon this, Aqeel deserted Ali and joined ranks with Muawiyah. In turn, Muawiyah gave him one hundred thousand dirham. Muawiyah insisted that Aqeel should declare from the pulpit the way Ali treated him. Aqeel climbed on the pulpit and addressed the gathering: "Listen, Ali preferred his faith to me and Muawiyah preferred me to his faith". [40]

Reorganization of *Zakah* and *Kharaj* Distribution

Immediately after becoming the caliph, Ali started reforming, reorganizing the management of public treasury in general, and accounts department in particular. He removed dishonest officers from their services. Ali reorganized the *zakah* based expenditure policy reflecting the essence of Quranic classification [9:60]. Since *zakah* is a faith-based levy, the Quran enumerates its beneficiaries. There is no scope either to increase or to decrease the number of beneficiaries. However, its administration can be reorganized to serve the very purpose of *zakah* levy in a meaningful way. This is what Ali did. *Zakah* proceeds were used as under:

1. Administration of the departments of collection and distribution of *zakah*.
2. Grants, donations and aid to poor, have-nots, orphans, aged, widows and disabled persons.
3. Honorarium to volunteers who fought for the state.
4. Pensions to widows and orphans of soldiers and officers of the army.
5. Acquiring and setting free the slaves from the bondage of slavery.
6. Reparation of government loans.
7. Helping pilgrims whenever and wherever they were found stranded.

As compared to the *zakah* levy, the beneficiaries of *kharaj* and *jiziyah* proceeds are not mentioned in the Quran. The righteous caliphs took advantage of this flexibility and the revenue was used for administrative and development purposes. *Kharaj* revenue came to the fore during the caliphate of Umar. He, in consultation with the companions of the Prophet, notably Ali, used *kharaj* for defence and development. Specifically, Ali earmarked revenue from *jiziyah* and *kharaj* for the following items of expenditure: [41]

1. Maintenance of army.
2. Construction and maintenance of forts.
3. Construction and maintenance of roads and bridges.
4. Sinking, maintenance and repairs of wells.
5. Construction of rest houses.

An essential point to note here is that the above-mentioned are 'secular heads' of expenditure. Both Muslims and non-Muslims are benefited. The *zakah* specific expenditure is, however, faith based.

On account of continuous internal disturbances, Ali shifted the seat of caliphate to Kufa. Thereat, he himself often supervised distribution of funds. Ali adopted a system of weekly distribution of public funds. Funds were distributed on every Thursday so that Muslims could happily spend their weekly holiday on Friday. Accounts were closed on every Thursday and every Saturday *bayt al maal* started with fresh books of accounts. [42] Abu Ubaid on the authority of Musa bin Tarif narrates that once Ali entered in *bayt al maal.* He had a disapproving glance at it and remarked: "By sun set I will not leave here a single dirham". He called a person from Bani Asad and asked him to distribute the entire collection. [43]

Once the distribution was over and accounts cleared, Ali would sweep and clean entire building of *bayt al maal*. He used to offer prayers in the *bayt al maal* itself, thanking his Lord that he had performed his duty faithfully. He used to address in these words: "Oh *bayt al maal* bear witness before Almighty that I have not withheld anything from Muslims". [44] Once he left his office empty handed. On that day, he had given his share to an old woman who complained that her share did not suffice her. Abu Ubaid reports that once after the completion of distribution of stipends, etc., Ali remarked that he has no right to keep *bayt al maal's* wealth accumulated. [45]

Strict Scrutiny of Public Officers

As in the case of Umar, Ali openly and publicly scrutinized the conduct of his officers. He never delayed any required action. Well before their appointments, Ali personally advised his officers regarding their conduct. Very often, he wrote letters to them emphasizing transparency in the collection and distribution of funds. *Nahjul Balagha* is full of such letters and instructions.

Earlier to Ali's ascension to the seat of caliphate, Muslim army had conquered Armenia a rich Central Asian country. Entire revenue from *khums* from Armenia was granted to

Marwan bin Hakam. After assuming caliphate, Ali did not approve the same. He handed back all these fiefs and estates to public exchequer. On that occasion he remarked: "By God if I had found that public money had been squandered even celebrating marriages and in purchasing slave-girls, I would have taken them back and would have handed over the country (public treasury), because functions and responsibilities of justice and equity are far-reaching and far extending". [46]

During the caliphate of Ali, Ashus bin Quais was the governor of Azerbaijan. When Ali learnt that the governor had amassed huge wealth, disproportionate to his known means, Ali issued a stern warning making clear to him the notion of *bayt al maal* and responsibilities of the governor. Ali said: "Verily you are not entrusted with the governorship that you may amass wealth. Neither it is tasty nor a juicy morsel to be swallowed...In your control and custody, there is one of the treasuries of God. You are only a treasurer; you have no right to make a personal use of any part of it. It is (your) duty to pass it on to those to whom it (really) belongs". [47] .

Similarly, Ali imprisoned the Governor of Ray who embezzled land revenue but he managed to escape to Muawiyah. The cases of fraud were not new. These were also reported in the caliphate of Umar but such criminals had no protection from any quarter. There were no alternative centres of power in the periods of Umar and Usman. Consequently, nobody dared to challenge the authority of the then Islamic state. However, by the time, Ali became caliph, the ground situation and outlook of people had drastically changed altering the power equations.

Ali has had an extra-ordinary concern for the management of public funds. He held that the public funds were reserved for poor, old, destitute, widows, orphans and paupers. He never allowed any officer to play with those funds. Once, one of his governors plundered public funds. [48] He felt sad that his governor did so at a time when Ali was seriously preoccupied with another engagement. He reprimanded him:

"You have invaded the public treasury and you looted as much as was possible for you, the money which was reserved for old widows, orphans and poor. Your action resembled the way wolf attacking and snatching away a wounded and helpless goat…money was earmarked for the use of orphans, paupers and destitute and it was reserved for the defence of Muslim state". [49]

Public Fund as Trust

Ali firmly held the view that public money belonged only to the poor who are its rightful owners. In this context, Ali wrote to one of his governors: "I advise you to fear God and return the money to those to whom it rightly belongs. If you do not do this, and if God gives me a chance to punish you, then I shall act in such a way that God will be pleased with me. I swear by God that had even Hassan and Hussain behaved in the way you behaved, I would not have shown indulgence to them; they could not have accepted any favour or consideration from me. I would have taken this money back from them and would have undone the harm done by them. I swear by the Merciful Lord that even if all the wealth which you have so sinfully looted had come into my possession in a lawful way, it would not have pleased me to leave it to my heir as an heirloom". [50]

Once one of his close companions, Abdullah bin Zumma, requested for some money from the public treasury. Ali replied: "The public treasury is neither my property nor yours. It is the property of Muslims, it is collected through their exertions (when they pay *zakah* out of their wealth, etc.) or it is booty of their wars. If you had joined them in the wars, you would also have received your share. What they have earned at the risk of their lives cannot be indiscriminately passed on to others". [51] This sermon once again clarifies Ali's perception of *bayt al maal*. Two things are very clear. First, the wealth deposited with *bayt al maal* is a public property and no one, not even caliph, has any special claim over it. Secondly, even the caliph cannot use it indiscriminately.

In the distribution of public funds, Ali was against favouring relatives and other members of his clan. His basic perception was that public wealth belonged to all and none should be favoured. In a letter to Muskala ibn Hoobayra, the governor of Ardsher Kharra, Ali writes: "I am given to understand that you are lavishly distributing state treasury among the Bedouins of your clan and among those desert Arabs who are faithful to you. You know this wealth has been gathered by faithful Muslims in the battlefields at the risk of their lives during wars in which many were killed and many more wounded. Do not imagine that the trust reposed by God in you can be treated lightly...Remember that all the Muslims, who are here and there, have an equal share in this wealth. Believing and acting on this principle, they come to me for their share and after receiving it from me they return to their places". [52]

Unfavourable Response

Ali's policy of equal distribution did not receive a favourable response. It was held as "too egalitarian". Ali was criticised on the ground that had he given preference to the chiefs of tribes and presented them with gifts as Muawiyah did, Ali would have earned loyalty of those chiefs. He would have established peace and prevailed over his opponents. But, Ali did not do that for the reason that loyalty to the faith was more important than the loyalty of a particular person or clan.

The Islamic state at the time of Ali had already expanded hugely. It was spread over millions of miles and hundreds and thousands of persons were its citizens. Purchasing people's loyalty with money meant that Ali had to pay tens and thousands of dinars to hundreds of the chiefs. Giving one chief would inflame the appetite of many other chiefs. Price of loyalty could have also gone very high. When Usman was endowing gifts and fiefs to his people, there was none to contest except a few verbal protests from Ali and others. Ali would have been surely contested by others in general and Muawiyah in particular. The eighth of the *zakah* and half of the fifth would not have been sufficient to satisfy the claims of tribal chiefs.

Another criticism levelled against Ali was that he did not compromise with the situations. Although such purchases were not permissible in the faith under normal circumstances, but were allowed under extraordinary circumstances. Here, Ali had had two options. The first one was to continue the path of equity and justice at the cost of his own life, power and caliphate. The second option was to sacrifice the principle of equity and justice and thereby strengthen his position and save his rule. These two, indeed, were competing options. Ali, as was expected from an upright person and a noble soul, favoured the policy of equity and justice at cost of his rule and life.

We have noted in the previous paragraphs that the public unrest was mainly due to a mishandling public finances and preferential allotment of vast lands. The common point between Ali and opponents of Usman was an equitable distribution of public funds. Had Ali not started reforming the policy, he would have met with the same fate, as that of Usman. History records that when Ali appointed Abdullah bin Abbas as the governor of Basra and his brother Obeidullah a governor of Yemen, Malik Al-Ashtar with all his loyalty to Ali resented saying: "Why did we kill the old man yesterday? [53] He meant to say that the uprising against Usman was caused by his policy of preference. What would have been the attitude of Malik al-Ashtar and others like him if Ali had tried to purchase loyalty of the chiefs of tribes and clans through public funds?

Thus, an objective assessment of the then prevailing situation would make it clear that Ali had to follow a policy of equal distribution of funds and drop the preferential treatment in appointing governors, officers and granting of fiefs. This, however, is incorrect to say that he had come under the pressure of rebels and assassins of Usman and effected a change in the policy. Even otherwise, in principle, Ali was not in favour of the policy of unequal distribution.

End Notes

1. Abu Ubaid, *Kitab al-Amwal*, op. cit., p. 60.
2. Please note that one jareeb of land is equal to 2268.75 square yards.
3. *Nahjul Balagha:* Letter No. 53, p. 502. See also Ziaul Haque's *Landlord and Peasant in Early Islam*, Islamic Research Institute, Islamabad, Pakistan, 1984, p. 40.
4. Ibid.
5. For a detailed discussion one may refer to Stephen J. Bailey's *Strategic Public Finance*, Palgrave MacMillan, 2004. Also, M.G. Rao and Mihir Rakshit (eds.) *Public Economics: Theory and Practice-Essays in Honour of Amaresh Bagchi*, Sage India, 2011.
6. The recent phenomenon of "Arab Spring" (2011) is a reflection of people's mood against the rule of despots.
7. Ibid.
8. *Nahjul Balagha*, p. 503.
9. Amini, Muhammad Taqi Amini, *The Agrarian System of Islam*, op. cit., p. 219.
10. *Kitab al-Amwal:* Narration No. 1804.
11. *Nahjul Balagha*, p. 503.
12. *Nahjul Balagha:* Letter No. 51.
13. *Kitab al-Amwal:* Narration No. 116 and *Kanzul Ummal:* Narration No. 1436.
14. Other famous canons of taxation are equity, efficiency, elasticity, simplicity and economy.
15. *Nahjul Balagah:* Letter No. 24.
16. *Nahjul Balagah:* Letter No. 24.
17. *Nahjual Balagha:* Letter No. 50.
18. *Nahjul Balagah:* Letter No. 24.
19. *Nahjul Balagah:* Letter No. 24.
20. There are several traditions of the Prophet that heavily denounce misappropriation and mismanagement of *zakah* funds. One may refer to narrations cited by Abu Ubaid.
21. *Nahjul Balagah:* Letter No. 25.
22. *Nahjul Balagha:* Letter No. 27.

23. *Nahjual Balagha:* Letter No. 50.
24. *Nahjul Balagha:* Letter No. 26.
25. Ibid.
26. Ibid.
27. Musgrave, Richard A. and Peggy B. Musgrave, *Public Finance in Theory and Practice*, Fifth Edition, Tata McGraw Hill, New Delhi, 2005, p. 9.
28. Rahman Afzal-ur, *Economic Doctrines of Islam* Vol. I, Islamic Publication Ltd., Lahore, 1980, pp. 125-126.
29. Al-Daudi, *Kitab al Kharaj,* op. cit., p. 64.
30. Siddiqui, M.N., *Islamic Public Economics,* op. cit., p. 116.
31. Nizami, Khaliq Ahmad, *Some Aspects of Religion and Politics in India During the Thirteenth Century,* op. cit., p. 18.
32. Al-Daudi, *Kitab al Kharaj,* op. cit., p. 107.
33. Rahman Afzal-ur, op. cit., pp.129 and 144.
34. Equal distribution did not mean equal amount. The people were given their share depending upon: (i) their efforts, and (ii) their familial requirements. "To each according to his/her needs" was the principle followed. No other consideration affected the policy of distribution. Certain measures per person were used.
35. For a detail discussion of this particular event, one may refer to the hadith collections of Imam Ahmad bin Hanbal, Tirmidhi, Nasa'i, Ibn Maja and Abu Dawud.
36. *Nahjul Balagha,* Sermon No. 19.
37. *Nahjul Balagha,* pp. 76-77.
38. *Nahjul Balagha,* Sermon No. 129.
39. *Tarikhul Khulfa,* p. 299.
40. Moududi, S.A.A., *Khilafat wa Malukiat*, op. cit., p. 75. And also *Tarikhul Khulfa*, p. 299.
41. *Nahjul Balagha,* p. 75.
42. The policy imperative is that there should be weekly payment in respect of poor because they find it difficult to wait for full one month on account of their deprivation. This idea also comes very close to zero-based budgeting.
43. *Kitab al-Amwal:* Narration No. 670.
44. *Kanzul Ummal:* Narration No. 36546.
45. *Kitab al-Amwal:* Narration No. 671.
46. *Nahjul Balagha:* Sermon No. 19.
47. *Nahjul Balagha,* Letter No. 5.
48. It is alleged that Ali's cousin Abdullah bin Abbass had once

behaved in this way.

49. *Nahjul Balagha,* Letter No. 41.
50. *Nahjul Balagha,* Letter No. 41.
51. *Nahjul Balagha,* Sermon No. 236.
52. *Nahjul Balagha,* Letter No. 4.
53. Chirri, M.J., *The Brother of the Prophet*, op. cit., p. 457.

6

Socio-Economic Concerns of Ali

Ali and Economic Security

The provision of economic security is associated with the welfare orientated of the state. The poor, marginalised and vulnerable sections of the society needs economic and social security the most. They do not have sufficient access to the market to procure their victuals. If not cared, these would be left to the mercy of market forces.

It was for the first time in the history of the religions of the world that Islam provided a political, social and economic space to the poor and marginalised. It institutionalised a regular help and assistance to the poor through *zakah* and *infaq*. It accorded a place of a tenet to the whole process of the transfer of funds in favour of poor. Islam designed and implemented a well-conceived delivery mechanism to ameliorate the status of poor. The Islamic shariah preferred that the state and its rulers should identify themselves with poor, needy and destitute.

We know that except a few, the Almighty Allah raised almost every prophet from amongst the poor. Almost every prophet identified himself with the poor. Helping and supporting the poor was, thus, a part of the prophetic mission. The Prophet quite often prayed: "O Allah, keep me alive as a destitute *(miskin)* and put me to death as a destitute and resurrect me in the group of the destitute". [1] What is meant here is that the destitution is a state of life where resources do not exceed the limits of self-sufficiency. It is also interpreted in the manner that the Prophet desired to become humble before Allah, the Exalted, and that he is raised, on the Day of Judgement, with poor. He also gave a glad tiding that poor will outnumber rich in the heaven.

Ali and His Poor Subjects

Ali hailed from a poor family. His father, Abu Talib bin Abdul Muttalib (549-619 C.E.), often found it difficult to support a large family. The public pronouncement of Islam and his association with the Prophet of Islam did not improve the economic condition of Ali. Even otherwise, Ali was of ascetic nature. When Ali became the caliph, he preferred the life of poverty to affluence. He led a life characterizing real traits of poverty. It was, therefore, natural that the poor and destitute were close to him.

During the regime of Ali, the poor always found a prime position, be it in his religious sermons, official instructions, letters, and public pronouncements. Notwithstanding the numerous civil wars, the poorest and downtrodden from amongst Muslims in general and "protected people" in particular, felt greatly safe and secured. They had not an iota of doubt about the distributive justice practiced by Ali. Justice, in its different forms, was not denied to any one and it was quickly delivered.

Certain heart-touching and soul-stirring episodes are cited here that make clear Ali's concern for the poor. Once a man came to Ali and said: "O Commander of Faithful, I am in need. I have already submitted it before the Almighty and now I am putting the same before you. If you attend to it, I will thank Allah and shower my praises on you. If not, I will still thank Allah and will excuse you". Ali replied: "Write it down on the ground for I do not like to see your face entreatingly". Thereafter, Ali gave him more than what he wanted, one hundred dinars and a pair of high quality dress. [2]

No one knew that Ali had provided a shelter to a leper in an advanced stage of that disease. The shelter was outside town, he used to go there daily, dress his wounds and feed him with his own hands because the leper had lost his fingers. He used to wash leper, put his bed in order and carry him out of the shelter for little time so that he may get fresh air. After the martyrdom of Ali, his relatives and friends came across this shelter and found a leper in it, learnt his history and told him that Ali was martyred and they had just buried him. Hearing the news and being unable to bear shock and grief, the poor leper died on the spot. [3]

Ali never missed any chance to impress upon people to help poor and needy. This, according to Ali, will be the best use of wealth, which he regarded as the trust from Almighty Allah. He remarks: "If God grants wealth and prosperity to any person, he should show kindness to his deserving kith and kin, should provide for the poor, should come the assistance of those are oppressed with calamities, misfortunes and reverses, should help the poor and have-nots and should assist honest people to liquidate their loans...". [4] This sermon also sheds light on the expenditure priorities set out by Ali during his period of caliphate.

In another heart touching Sermon, Ali pleads: "Beware! That if anybody finds poverty, destitution and starvation among his people and refuses to extend a helping hand, he will not add to his wealth by such means while expenditure on charity will neither decrease his wealth nor reduce him to poverty. He, who refrains from helping his people, must remember that he has withheld one hand of help and, at the time of his need, thousands of hands will abstain from his help". [5]

Pro-Poor Government

Ali wanted that his government should be pro-poor and it should sensitize issues relating to poverty and sufferings of masses. [6] At present in a large number of Muslim countries where poverty is rampant, people silently suffer from hunger, disease, malnutrition and deprivation of different types. [7] These phenomena may be attributed to several reasons, the major being lack of committed public action and public authorities.

Under the present circumstances, Muslim countries and governments should set the goal of realizing Ali's extraordinary vision. He had instructed his governor Malik al-Ahstar: "*When poor cannot reach you, you must reach the poor.* That nation or government cannot achieve salvation where the rights of depressed, destitute and suppressed are not guarded and where mighty and powerful persons are not forced to accede these rights". [8]

This pro-poor role of the government was advocated and practiced at a time when poor and deprived were left to the mercy of nature to fend for themselves. They never found any place in public agenda. In the present day secular economies, it is a very recent phenomenon that the governments have started responding to the needs of poor and vulnerable sections. Till the first half of 20th century, governments across the world were apathetic towards poor for the reason that they were still under the hangover of the policy of laissez faire and efficiency of market forces. They had a firm belief in the effectiveness of invisible hand, an idea propounded by Adam Smith.

A few developments in the beginning of twentieth century, however, paralyzed invisible hand, if not fully at least partly. These developments made governments to change their stance. [9] This shift in the policy was out of compulsion and not because of their real concern for poor and needy. The rich, because of income-consumption inequalities, had failed to generate a desired level of "effective demand", sufficient to support a warranted level of output, income and employment.

Apathetic governments lose their welfare character. Normally, even now, poor are afraid of approaching to the governments fearing force and torture. The administrative formalities and procedural delays also depress the poor. They hesitate, fearing repression, to raise voices against public authorities. Sensing this particular disability of poor, Ali instructed Malik al-Ashtar to 'reach to the poor'. This advice contains a strong pro-poor message.

Ali was very much concerned about the perception of poor. It is again evident from his letter to Malik Ashtar: "Remember that displeasure and disapproval of common men, have-nots and depressed persons more than overbalances the approval of important persons and displeasure of a few big will be excused by the Lord if the general public and masses of your subjects are happy with you. The common men, the poor, apparently less important sections of your subjects are the pillars of Islam...be more friendly with them and secure their confidence and sympathy". [10]

In respect of poor, deprived and disabled persons, Ali writes to Malik Ashtar "it is *absolutely* necessary that they should be looked after, helped and well provided for". [11] Here, Ali is emphasising the need for socio-economic support to the poor. In the same letter at a different place, Ali writes: "Then I want to caution you about the poor. Fear God about their conditions and your attitude toward them. They have no support, no resources, and no opportunities. They are poor, they are destitute, many of them are cripples, and unable to work. You should be a source of comfort, love and respect to them. Appoint a respectable, honest and pious person, a person who fears God, and can treat them respectfully, order him to find out everything about them and to bring the report to you". [12]

There is another long and a classic letter from Ali written to Usman bin Hunaif, his trusted governor of Basra province. It appears from the letter that poverty was rampant and Ali was aware of the sufferings of poor. There were people who were unable to have a piece of bread. He writes: "If I had so wanted I could have very easily found ways and means to provide for myself the purest and clearest honey, the best variety of wheat and finest silk clothes that could be woven. But is it not possible for inordinate cravings to overcome me, and it is not possible that greediness persuades me to acquire the choicest of victuals when in Hejaz [13] and Yemen, there may be people who have no hope of obtaining a piece of bread and who have never satisfied their hunger fully. It is not possible for me to satiate myself when there are people around me whom hunger and thirst keep restless and writhing. Do you want me to be like a person about whom somebody has very aptly said: "Is this disease not enough for you that you keep on sleeping on a very heavy stomach and around you there are such starving mouths that they will greedily eat even dried goat-skin". [14]

In the same letter, Ali in clear words identifies himself with the poor and weak. "Shall I be content and satisfied simply because people call me *Amir-ul-Momineen* (commander of faithful)? Shall I not sympathize with the faithful Muslims in their calamities? Shall I not be their partner in their adversities? Shall I not be their fellow in suffering? Shall I not set an example for them to patiently, courageously, bravely and virtuously bear up hardships and bereavements? [15] He later on proceeds to ask certain questions to himself. By doing so, he is asking questions to other persons in power during in his own times and in years to come. For example:

1. Am I created simply to keep on thinking about my food?
2. Am I like that animal which is tied down to a post and which thinks of nothing but its fodder?
3. Am I like that uncontrolled beast which roams about, does nothing but to eat, and does not know the purpose of life for which it is created?
4. Have I no religion, no conscience and no fear of the God?

While reminding Usman bin Hunaif about his regular duties towards the poor and weak, Ali warns him: "You have seen sheep and goats, after having their full they retire to their dens and sleep their lives away, do you want Ali ibn Abu Talib to be like them to eat, drink and enjoy? O Ibn Hunaif! Fear God and be content with the bread that you get with lawful means so that you may be exempted and freed from the fire of the hell? [16]

On one occasion, Usman bin Hunaif expressed his reservation over Ali's policy of out-reaching to the poor. He warned Ali that the poor and destitute were too poor to help Ali during any crisis. On his part, Ali rejected reservations of Usman bin Hunaif. He made his pro-poor stand still clearer.

He remarked: "As far as the usefulness of services of these disabled persons and have-nots is concerned, remember that I am not helping them to secure their services; I fully know they are unable to serve me. I help them because they cannot help themselves and they are as much human beings as you and I. May God help me to do my duty as He wishes me to do". [17]

Realizing the sufferings of poor, Ali asks rich people to pay *zakah* honestly and if need be they should pay more than the stipulated. Abu Ubaid, while discussing the payment of *zakah* beyond the prescribed rates, quotes Ali who remarked, "Allah has made it obligatory on wealthy people to pay so much of the *zakah* that suffices the needs of poor and destitute. The rich are mainly responsible if poor and needy happen to remain hungry and scarcely clad. They withhold poor's due. Now, it is Allah's turn to take them to task and punish them". [18] From this narration, we can deduce that Ali was in favour of excess *zakah* payment in the event of rampant poverty and sufferings of common men.

It was in the favour of public that Ali renounced his share in *khums*. Ali held his own view in the distribution of *khums*. Scholars have differed about the modality of the division of one-fifth of the booty *(al-khums)*. The rightly guided caliphs, except Ali, divided *khums* according to one's personal discretion *(ijtihad)* and not according to the number of groups of people mentioned in the Quranic verse. Ali's view and the opinion of Banu Hashim was that the *khums* was to be divided among five groups.

It is reported that Ali said: "I asked the Messenger of Allah to give me one-fifth of the fifth so that nobody could dispute with me in that". [19] And, the Prophet did accordingly. This continued till the end of the caliphate of Umar. Ali added: "I then said to Umar: 'This is needed by the general public while we do not need it, so, please distribute it among them'. Ali continued: "When I came out, al-Abbas, who was a farsighted person, said to me: 'You have taken out from our hands something which will never come back to us'. Ali said: 'I was not invited to it (i.e., to receive *khums*) afterwards". [20] The important point in this narration is that Ali of his own renounced his due share in *khums* on the ground that 'the general public need it and we do not need it'. Although Ali was never well-off in true sense of the term, yet he considered himself as well-off. This was mainly because of his esoteric contentment.

These instructions clearly show the direction in which Ali wanted to take the state under his rule. He wanted that his government should not be the one wherein officers enjoyed undue benefits at the cost of public money. He disapproved that rich should be allowed to get richer at the cost of injustice and inequity to the poor. He did not favour that the poor should be left to fend for themselves and become poorer because of their disabilities on one hand and apathetic and indifferent government and its officers on the other.

Ali and His Protectorates *(ahlu az-zimmah)*

Ali was very much particular about treatment meted out to the *ahlul z-zimmah*. The historical covenants were never violated. [21] There were express orders from Ali that no *jiziyah* should be collected from persons falling in the following categories" [22]

1. Those who were above 50 years of age.
2. Those who were below 20 years of age
3. All women folks.
4. All paralytic persons.
5. All disabled persons.
6. All blind persons.
7. All mentally retarded persons.

Exemption Nos. 1 and 2 make it clear that the protected people in the age group 20-50 only were taxed. When we study these two exemptions along with other exemptions, it is clear that a significant portion of protected people might have been outside the *jiziyah* net.

Abu Ubaid, on the authority of Antara, narrates that Ali

used to collect *jiziyah* in cash and where possible in-kind too. Abu Ubaid comments that this was because of the soft attitude of Ali towards the 'protected people'. He said: "Their goods are like ours, and bloods are like our bloods". This remark makes clear the universally tolerant nature of Islam. "The pleasant rains irrigate the fields of the people irrespective of their religion and community. Likewise, the benefaction of the Islamic rule is the common heritage of all human beings. The means and opportunities of progress are equally provided to all. The caliphate makes no distinction between theirs, and ours because all are slaves of Allah and, according to the Islamic viewpoint, subsistence of all is Allah's responsibility. The caliphate is His Vicegerency and bound to act under His commands. As such the responsibility of helping His creatures rests with the caliphate". [23]

Against Distress Sale

Ali did not force the *ahlul z-zimmah* to sell their articles/produce to clear *jiziyah*. [24] This would have caused a 'distress sale' forcing the sellers to sell their produce at low prices, which definitely would have been an unjust practice. Moreover, Ali was against any form of injustice. Similarly, when someone amongst 'protected people' embraced Islam, Ali exempted him from paying *jiziyah* but treated the land as 'crown land' and started collecting *kharaj*. [25]

Ali's humane approach is more visible when we go through the following instruction to one of his governors: "The protected people (*ahlu az-zimmah*) have reported of a canal which is choked up in your jurisdiction, and the Muslims are bound to repair it. You should inspect the site along with them and get the work done. To me improving and developing lands is preferable to having the inhabitants desert them". [26] Ali reiterated his belief once again that the improvement of lands is an area of prime concern. He was not in favour of people leaving their lands. Here, Ali derives home a point that as a rule the governments should not heavily tax persons, their professions and callings, their assets, etc., which force people to abandon their places and professions.

Once, a group of protected people complained against Abdullah Ibn Abbas that he had treated them with contempt and scorn. Ali wrote: "I deliberated about their complaints and about the situation and found that that if on account of their heathenism they do not deserve any favourable treatment of extra privileges yet they do not deserve to be treated insultingly, cruelly and harshly. They are governed by us, they have made certain agreements with us and we are obliged to respect and honour the terms of those agreements. Therefore, you in future be kind to them, tolerate them and give them due respect...Treat them as they individually deserve, kindly or harshly and with respect or with contempt". [27]

End Notes

1. Al-Dawudi, *Kitab al-Amwal,* op. cit., p. 201.
2. *Kanzul Ummal:* Narration No. 17146.
3. *Nahjul Balagah,* p. 22.
4. *Nahjul Balagah*, Sermon No. 145.
5. *Nahjul Balagah,* Sermon No. 28.
6. Under the circumstances that are prevailing in Muslim countries today, governments should set the goal of realizing Ali's vision.
7. For a detailed study of deprivation of different types, one may refer to various issues of *Human Development Report.* It has pointed out that there are three types of deprivation: (i) Survival deprivation; (ii) knowledge deprivation, and (iii) decent standard of living deprivation. One may also refer to various publications brought out by Mahbub ul-Haq Human Development Centre.
8. *Nahjul Balagha*, p. 506.
9. Major developments were: (i) The Russian Revolution of 1917, (ii) the Great Depression of 1929 and (iii) publication of Keynes' *General Theory*. The first provided political shock, the second provided economic shock and the third development generated academic shock damaging the old notion of non-intervention.
10. Ibid.
11. *Nahjul Balagha*, p. 499.
12. *Nahjul Balagha*, p. 505.
13. Hejaz, also spelled Hedjaz, Arabic Al-Ḥijāz, a region of western

Saudi Arabia, along the mountainous Red Sea coast of the Arabian Peninsula from Jordan on the north to Asir region on the south.

14. *Nahjul Balagha,* Letter No. 45.
15. Ibid.
16. *Nahjul Balagha,* Letter No. 45.
17. *Nahjul Balagha,* pp. 76-77.
18. *Kitab al-Amwal:* Narration No. 1909. Also, *Kanzul Ummal:* Narration No. 16840.
19. Al-Dawudi, Abu Jafar Ahmad ibn Nasr, *Kitab al-Amwal,* Islamic Research Institute, Islamabad, Pakistan, 1995, p. 54.
20. Ibid.
21. Some of the historical covenants were with Najranites, with the people of Fidak, with the people of Aila, with the people of suburban areas of Madinah, with the clan of Juhaina, clan of Ashja, Khuzaa, Aslam, Qadhaa and Adra, etc. For further details, one may refer to Muhammad Taqi Amini's *Agrarian System of Islam,* Idarah-e-Adbiyat-e-Dilli, Delhi, 1991.
22. *Nahjul Balagha:* Letter No. 26.
23. Amini, Muhammad Taqi, *The Agrarian System of Islam,* Idarah-e-Adbiyat-e-Dilli, Delhi, 1991. For a better understanding of the whole issue one may refer to A.R. Momin's *Islam and Pluralism,* Jamia Hamdard, New Delhi, 2004. Also Arshi Khan's "Islam, Tolerance and Pluralism", *Indian Journal of Secularism,* Vol. 16, No. 1, April-June, 2012, pp. 50-90.
24. *Kitab al-Amwal:* Narration Nos. 117 and 957.
25. *Kitab al-Amwal:* Narrations Nos. 123, 124, 206 and 234. And also, Al-Jassas's *Al ahkam al Quarn,* Vol. III, p. 532.
26. Hasan uz Zaman S.M., *The Economic Functions of the Early Islamic State,* op. cit., p. 311.
27. *Nahjul Balagha,* Letter No. 19, pp. 442-443.

7

Ali and Governance

No Room for Disorder and Anarchy

The need for the establishment of state and its different organs arises from the fact that Islam is against an unorganized and undisciplined way of life. Islam directs its followers not only in the matters of worship and material transactions but it demands a political and administrative organization in accordance with the directions of the Prophet, through whom the will of God is revealed to all. Islam rejects the western concept of separation of church from the state and *vice versa.*

The Holy Quran condemns disorder and anarchy and warns of a grievous penalty to those engaged in creating disturbances. The need for the state, an embodiment of authority, arises to check perfidious activities. The Quran directs: "O ye believe! Obey God and obey the Apostle, and those charged with authority among you. If ye differ in anything among yourselves, refer it to God and His Apostle, if ye believe in God and the last Day; that is the best and most suitable for final determination" (4:59).

According to this verse, the people are required to obey the commands of God, His Messenger and "those in authority". What is meant here is that "those in authority" are neither the God nor the Prophet, they are ordinary mortals. Yet, the God commands obedience to them in the interest of peaceful public life. In this context, it is necessary on the part of rulers to rule according to the will and wish of the God. They are required to respect the "trust" with which they are charged. Now it is the turn of the people that they should respect the Divine Command about obeying the *wali al-'amr,* (person in authority) and respond to his call.

The Islamic shariah regards the head of state as a trustee

and a guardian; it regards just governance as a fulfilment of a trust entrusted to the ruler. The Prophet of Islam stressed the need for a proper and orderly organization. There is a popular tradition according to which the Prophet said: "If (as few as) three persons go on a journey, they must appoint one out of themselves as their leader".

The Prophet succeeded in building an organized society whose essential feature was compactness. The Prophet did not intend to set himself as a head of state nor did his predecessors aspire. His mission was to bring back people to the rightly guided path. It was, however, the vicious and violent opposition to the prophetic mission that forced the Prophet to lay the foundation of an Islamic state as a means of protecting his followers and their faith. The Prophet took upon himself the responsibility of a ruler that was not at all his aim. There was neither a crown, a throne nor any palace.

During the battle of Uhud (625 C.E.), when the Muslims were defeated, a rumour spread that the Holy Prophet had been killed. Depressed and dejected, a group of his followers fled from the battlefield. Referring to this incident, the Quran says: "Muhammad is no more than an apostle; many were the apostles that passed away before him. If he died or were slain will ye then turn back on your heels? If any did turn back on his heels, not the least harm will he do to God; but God (on the other hand) will swiftly reward those who (serve Him) with gratitude" (3:144)". It is clear from the above verse:

1. If the Messenger is killed in a battle, it should not in any way stall, even temporarily, the struggle against evil forces.
2. There is no question of turning back. The struggle should continue under the command of an able and trustworthy.
3. If the Prophet is killed or if he is dead, the social system and military organization of the Muslims should not disintegrate.

From this, one may infer to what extent the Quran and the Prophet regarded as harmful the disorder and absence of an authority amongst Muslims. A leader is necessary to push forward the prophetic mission. His presence is necessary to resolve social conflicts and to serve as a unifying link among Muslims.

The words *ra'i* for the ruler and *ra'iyyah* for the masses first appear in the traditions of the Prophet. These words are derived from the root *ra'a,* which carries the sense of 'protection' and 'safeguarding'. A tradition of the Prophet throws light on the meaning of this word: "Truly, every one of you is a *ra'i* responsible for his *rai'yyah*. The ruler is the *ra'i* of his people and responsible for them; the woman is the *ra'i* of her husband's house and responsible for it; the slave is the *ra'i* of his master's property and responsible for it; indeed all of you are *ra'i* and responsible for those under your charge".

Ali on Need for the Government and its Benefits

In this context, Ali identifies three attributes of a good ruler. [1] First, the ruler should be very just; secondly, he should not put a veil between himself and his people and thirdly, should impose the dictates of Allah on every one without regard to the relation or family links. In order words, Ali is emphasizing fact that a ruler should avoid partisan attitude and he should be close to his people as much as possible.

Nahjul Balagha deals with numerous issues concerning the state and social justice. Ali repeatedly stressed the need for a powerful and benevolent government, and, in his own time, battled against the views propagated by the *khawarij* (secedors). The slogan of the *khawarij* was *"la hukm illa li Allah*", (there is no command but God's) a phrase adopted from the Holy Quran. Its Quranic meaning is that the prerogative of legislation belongs to God or those whom God has permitted to legislate. However, the *khawarij* interpreted it differently. Ali was of the opinion that they had imparted a false sense to a true statement. [2]

"The slogan which they keep on repeating is in itself a

truth but they deduce wrong meaning and infer conclusions out of it (which are) harmful to the mankind. Yes! There can be no law and no order but that of God; but they infer that none should be the king or ruler over mankind but God. How it is possible? Necessarily, there ought to be some form of government. There ought to be human agency as a ruler; this may either be a pious and benevolent ruler or any ungodly government". [3]

After making the above remarks, Ali explains the benefits flowing from a kind and benevolent government. "A benevolent and godly government is necessary so that under its kind rule, Muslims and non-Muslims alike may prosper and enjoy fruits of the efforts of their mind and body; that under its benign protection God may grant them happy life and peaceful end; that under its auspicious governance they may flourish and thrive; that under its banner they may defend themselves against enemies; that there may be safety on highways and security of life, honour, religion and hereafter; and that the rights and claims of poor, humble, depressed may be secured for them from the grasps of rich and powerful oppressors so that virtuous people may be protected from molesters and vicious sinners". [4]

Based upon the above statement of Ali, we derive the following universal benefits from a benevolent government:

1. A benevolent government helps its citizens, both Muslims and non-Muslims to prosper.
2. It helps people to realize the fruits of their mental and physical work.
3. A benevolent government ensures peace and security by protecting borders of the country.
4. It ensures safety on highways, the wayfarers feel protected.
5. It protects honour, religion and faith of its people. Their dignity is safeguarded.
6. It empowers poor, depressed and weak persons and prevents their exploitation by the rich.

7. It curbs the sinners from further petrifying the social and moral fiber of the society.
8. It reigns in the powerful oppressors so that poor and virtuous are protected from being assaulted and exploited by vicious sinners.

In *Kanzul Umaal* there is a narration similar to the above. Ali said: "only a ruler, good or bad, can set right the things. People enquired: "We can understand this in case of a God fearing ruler. But, how come an impious ruler? Ali replied that it is through the impious ruler that the Almighty protects highways; under his command, battles against enemies can be fought; war booty can be obtained; commands of Allah may be imposed through him; *haj* can be performed under his lead; Muslims are able to worship Allah peacefully. Whatever may be his conduct, he is a source of comfort and protection to the people". [5] When Ali realized that the situation was slipping from under his control, he is reported to have remarked that "I fear, shortly Muawiyah will overpower you". His followers asked: "Should we not wage battle against him? He replied: "There must be a ruler, pious or impious". [6]

Ali on Government's Vision and Mission

A study of *Nahjul Balagha* makes it clear that Ali was sensitive to the issues related to the government and justice. He considers them to be of paramount importance. The Quran declares: "Indeed, We sent Our messengers with the clear signs, and We sent down with them the Book and the Balance so that men might uphold justice" (57:25). This verse declares the establishment of justice as a major objective of the mission of all the prophets. Hence, how was it possible that someone like Ali, whose duty was to expound the teachings of the Quran and explain the doctrines and laws of Islam, might have ignored this issue or, at least, accorded it a secondary importance?

On an occasion when Ali was marching toward Basra, Ali along with Abdullah ibn Abbas stopped at Ziquar. Abdullah ibn Abbas found Ali putting stitches to and repairing his very old worn out shoes. Ali asked ibn Abbas: "What do you think would be the cost of this pair of shoes? He replied: "Nothing Sir! Not even the cost of stitches put on them. They are worthless". Ali replied: "Ibn Abbas if I cannot establish a regime of justice and truth and if cannot eradicate tyranny and impiety, then the value of this caliphate is less to me than the cost of this pair of shoes". [7] Thus, according to Ali the mission of caliphate is accomplished only when: (a) a regime of justice and truth is established, and (b) tyranny and impiety are checked. Ali is reported to have remarked: "I am thankful to Allah for having selected me (as the caliph) for this service (to the poor). Further, attending to the needs of poor and destitute is more valuable to me than the entire deposits of gold and silver on this earth". [8]

The vision of Ali was to establish rule of Allah over His bondsmen. Throughout his rule, Ali demonstrated that the values of Islam would not be sacrificed for the sake of administrative needs and exigencies of political situation. "The Caliph was first and foremost, a missionary of Islam, an ideal of Islamic morality to the people than merely a head of the state. Ali was determined to abide by this principle by giving it priority over all other administrative and political considerations, irrespective of the cost he might have to pay for it. He actually did pay a heavy price for upholding this principle. And he did it willingly with a clear conscience". [9]

Reciprocity of Rights and Duties

There is a sermon of Ali discussing rights and duties of the rulers and ruled wherein he condemns flattery, sycophancy and advices his people not to flatter the men in power to serve their interests. Recognizing mutual rights, Ali speaks out: "The Almighty God by entrusting your affairs to me has given me a right over you. And, as I have right over you so you have a right over me". [10] In connection with rights of the Creator and His creatures, he speaks: "Between the two persons one has right over the other only when the latter has rights over the former. One-sided obligation is possible only with God. He has rights over His creatures but they in return have no rights. This is His privilege". [11]

There is a similar narration in *Kitab al Amwal.* Musaeeb bin Saad reports that Ali, glorifying the truth, said: "It is the duty of the Imam that he should deliver justice in accordance with the commands of Allah and protect the trust (of the God and people). If he is so acting, it is fundamentally necessary upon people to listen to him, obey him and respond to his call". [12]

Ali enumerates certain benefits when people recognize mutual rights and duties. For example, these benefits are: [13]

1. Truth and piety will prevail in the society.
2. Traditions of the Prophet will be accepted and acted upon.
3. Religion will be firmly established.
4. Equity and justice will be order of the day.
5. Civilization will experience progress.
6. Wealth will not be accumulated using unfair means.

Ali is careful enough to add here the inherent dangers in not exercising mutual respect in the matters of rights. "But when subjects revolt against their ruler without any justifiable cause and undermine his authority, or when the ruler oppresses, tyrannizes, exploits and deprives them of their natural or acquired rights, then differences will creep in...". [14] Obviously, he anticipated the following dangers: [15]

1. Law and order will receive a setback.
2. Despotism will be order of the day.
3. Religious practices will be ignored, canons of religion will be disrespected and disregarded.
4. Inordinate desires will rule human minds.
5. Pious and good people will be dishonoured and disgraced; wicked people will be honoured and respected. [16]
6. Wrath of the God will descend on the people in one way or the other.

Fundamental Functions of the Government

We must study Ali's letters to his governors, especially those that were meant to be the official circulars. It is in these letters that we find glimpses of the teachings of Islam on the topics of functions of the head of state and his duties toward the people as well as their rights. These letters also help in developing a personal profile of Ali as a model head of state, keen to serve his subjects with love, affection, justice and use force where necessary. In this regard, his letter to Malik al-Ashtar has a unique place in the history of official letters of Muslim caliphs and rulers.

Malik Al-Ashtar [17] (d. 658 C.E.) was one of the most loyal companions of Ali. Al-Ashtar embraced Islam during the Prophet's time, and rose to prominence during the caliphates of Usman and Ali. During the caliphate of Ali, he fought in the Battle of Jamal (656 C.E.) and Siffin (657 C.E.). He was recognized for his fierce and steadfast defence of Islam in different battles as well as his pious nature. After the Battle of Siffin, he was appointed as the governor of Egypt in 658 C.E. (38 A.H.) Earlier to him Muhammad bin Abu Bakr (631-658 C.E.) was the governor of Egypt who was martyred at the prime age of 27 years.

Ali wrote a long letter to Malik al-Ashtar explaining the Islamic principles of administration and justice. The issues highlighted in this letter are: fear of God; that the government is of God; the governors and the governed are both creatures of God; their respective duties are laid down by God; the orphans and deprived are trust of God; and the army is the army of God. A famous Christian scholar of Arab origin, Abdul Maseeh Anthaki, is reported to have remarked: "(This letter) explains what a humane administration should be like and how it is to be carried on. It justifies the claims of Muslims that Islam wants to introduce a Godly administration of the people, for the people and by the people and it wants that a ruler should rule not to please himself but to bring happiness to the ruled. Ali should be congratulated for having introduced these principles in his government and for having written them down for posterity". [18]

In the preamble of the letter, Ali writes: "In the name of Allah, the Merciful and Kind God. These are the orders issued by the creature of God, Ali, the son of Abu Talib, to Malik, when he appointed Malik as the Governor of Egypt to collect *zakah* there, to fight against the enemies of Islam and the Egypt, to work for the welfare of its people and look after its prosperity". [19] From this preamble, we can deduce Ali's perspective of governorship. In his opinion the duties of the governor are:

1. To collect *zakah* and other such levies from the eligible persons.
2. To protect the faith of Islam from its enemies.
3. To protect Egypt from foreign aggressions.
4. To promote the welfare of its people.
5. To ensure the prosperity of its people.

An in between line reading of the above mentioned duties of governor makes it abundantly clear that the protection of Islam and Egypt goes side by side ensuring protection to all its people without regard to their religion. Similarly, welfare of people and their prosperity through the fight against poverty also assumes a secular character. In the opinion of Ali, the Islamic state should not make any difference between Muslims and non-Muslim and two should be treated with equity and justice. Ali warns Malik Ashtar in these words: "I order you to use your head, heart, hands and tongue to help (creatures) of God because the Almighty God holds Himself responsible to help those who sincerely try their best to help Him (in His cause and His creatures)". [20]

The just and equitable approach of Ali is clear when the following instruction is read: "Remember Malik that amongst your subjects there are two types of people: those who are having same religion as your and they are brothers unto you and those who have other religion than yours and yet they are human beings like. Men of the either category suffer from the same weaknesses and disabilities that the human flesh is heir to. Let your mercy and compassion come to their rescue and help in the same way and to the same extent that you expect God to show mercy and forgiveness to you". [21] Ali, thus, tags the Mercy of God and His Forgiveness to a kind treatment that the head of state should extend to all under his rule.

This very much resembles to a prophetic tradition where the Prophet is reported to have remarked "if a person, whom the Almighty Allah as made a ruler, is not a well-wisher of people, he would not then come even near to the fragrance of heaven". And also "A ruler will not enter into heaven with the Prophet who despite holding a responsible position was neither the well wisher of people nor worked for their welfare". [22]

Since the subjects of the state suffer from certain common weaknesses, Ali warns Malik Ashtar in these words: "Do not hurry over punishment...do not get angry and lose your temper quickly over the mistakes and failures of those over whom you rule. Never say to yourself: I am their lord, their ruler and all in all over them and that I must be obeyed submissively and humbly". [23]

Conduct of Governors

In one of the letters of Ali, it appears: "Verily you are not trusted with the governorship that you may amass wealth, neither it is tasty nor a juicy morsel to be swallowed. On the contrary, it is trust committed to your care and faith. Its responsibility lies upon your shoulders. Your *Amir* has appointed you as a shepherd and guardian of the people. You have no right to do, as you like and to act independently without seeking his (*amir's*) advice and authority. In important affairs of the state and the public, your decisions must be based on facts and sound reasons". [24]

We already know that Ali was very particular in respect of *bayt al maal*. He was worried about its misuse. He never lost an opportunity to reprimand governors and other officers regarding sanctity of *bayt al maal*. Ali equates *bayt al maal* as a treasure of God. He instructs: "In your control and custody there is one of the treasures of God, you are only a treasurer, you have no right to make a personal use of any part of this wealth, it is your duty to pass it on to those whom it belongs. I hope you will not give me a chance to prove myself a hard taskmaster and a harsh lord for you. May you see the light". [25]

Ali repeatedly reminded his governors to be kind, generous and gracious to their subjects. He was against using harsh measures to reform people and to establish rule over them. He advised his governors to win over the hearts of people and thereby seek their cooperation. He writes: "In your treatment with the subjects, remember that you should use leniency and tolerance along with severity. Be kind, tolerant and lenient as far as and as long as possible but when you feel that your aims cannot be achieved without severity, rigidity and harshness, only then you can adopt such an attitude". [26]

Composition of Advisory Council

Ali has also spoken about the need for an advisory council to support and assist the head of state. Before becoming Caliph, Ali rendered his advice to Abu Bakr, Umar and Usman, where necessary. Sincerity, sagacity and farsightedness were hallmarks of his advice. Ali advised the commoners too.

Ali instructed Malik al-Ashtar that he should not appoint misers, cowards and greedy persons as advisors. He should not allow them to intervene into the affairs of the state. They appear to be well-wishers but it is just their pretension. Ali has justified his stand by speaking about their inherent qualities. A common attribute of them all is that they do not have a perfect faith and trust in God. He writes: "Do not accept advice of misers, they will try their best to keep you away from acts of kindness and from doing good to others. They will keep you frightening from poverty and destitution.

Similarly, do not allow cowards and weaklings to act as

your advisers because they will make you timid in issuing and enforcing your orders, will terrify you to handle important affairs boldly and will make your enterprises and invasions timid and timorous attempts. At the same time, avoid greedy and covetous persons. Remember that miserliness, cowardice and greed appear to be different wicked qualities but they all arise from the same evil mentality of having no faith and no trust in God. Your worst ministers will be the men who had been a minister to the tyrannical and oppressive rulers before you and who had been a party to atrocities and savage cruelties committed by them". [27]

Typology of People

For the purpose of smooth administration of the state, Ali instructed Malik Ashtar to divide people into the following categories:

1. Army personnel who defend the cause of God.
2. Secretaries of the state who issue general or special orders on the direction of caliph/governor.
3. Judges and magistrates who administer justice.
4. Officers maintaining law and order, guarding the peace and prosperity of the country.
5. Common people, both Muslims and non-Muslims, who pay taxes.
6. Professionals and artisans.
7. Poor and have-nots. [28]

It is very interesting to note that this classification is based on two major considerations. First, the faith (Muslims and non-Muslims) and secondly, professions and callings. There is no mention of caste, creed and colour. It is also not done on the basis of wealth or social status of a person. As usual, the poor and deprived find a place in the above-mentioned classification.

After categorizing people into different groups, Ali remarks that all these represent a closely woven net. They are all dependent upon one another. He writes: "...the prosperity or welfare of each class of the society, individually and collectively, is so interdependent upon the wellbeing of the other classes...one class cannot exist peacefully, cannot live happily and cannot work without the support and good wishes of the other...The Merciful Lord has fixed rights and duties of each one of them which have been either given out in His Book and or explained through the orders and traditions of the Holy Prophet, a complete code of which is preserved with us". [29]

In the context of the maintenance of army, Ali speaks of importance of tax collection: "The upkeep and maintenance of an army depends upon the taxes collected by the state out of which God hath fixed for them a share. With this amount they provide their requirements, maintain themselves and their arms in fit position to fight for religion and cause of justice". [30] In this instruction, Ali is referring to Verse 60 of Chapter 9 of the Holy Quran.

After explaining need, significance and interdependence of each class, Ali asks Malik Ashtar to be sincere in his rule, which should be based upon the principles of equity and justice. This sincerity will generate love and respect amongst masses: "Remember Malik! Almighty God will not absolve any ruler of the obligations laid upon him unless he sincerely tries his best to discharge duties, prays the Lord to help him in their acquittal, remains steadily and diligently on the path of truth and justice and bears all this whether the performance of these duties is congenial to him or hateful...The things which should gladden the heart of a ruler must be the fact that his state is being ruled on the principles of equity and justice and that his subjects love him. And, your subjects will love you only when their hearts are not sore against you". [31]

Types of Rulers

In the opinion of Ali, there are only two types of rulers. "One is God fearing, sincere, diligent and taking right action at the right time and place. He follows the principles of justice and equity and protects the rights of others. He is not the one who takes shelter behind gorgeous curtains, show of pomp and pride. The other is one who is utterly apathetic to the needs of ruled and leads a life ostentation and extravagance. He fails in meeting his private and public obligations". [32] Ali then repeatedly asks Malik Ashtar to be a sincere and God-fearing ruler.

Ali was aware of previous rules and rulers over Egypt and elsewhere where men in charge of public affairs generously rewarded their kith and kin at the expense of rightful and deserving persons. Their partial attitude ultimately led to downfall of the once mighty empires. Taking this particular fact into consideration, Ali warns Malik Ashtar in these words: "So far as your own affairs and those of your relatives and friends are concerned take care that you do not violate the duties laid down upon you by the God and usurp the rights of mankind, be impartial (in granting fiefs and delivering justice) and do justice...nothing will bring down His vengeance and His anger quicker than to insist upon oppression and tyranny over His creatures. [33]

As it is well known, Ali led a very simple life, ate minimum of simple food, wore very simple clothes, and used worn out shoes. He knew it well that his governors will not replicate his standard, yet he advised them to lead a life devoid of pomp and extravagance. In this context, he writes: "Do not place a prestige curtain between you and those over whom you rule. Such pretensions and show of pomp and pride are in reality manifestations of inferiority complex and vanity". [34] Ali quotes the Prophet who said: "From Allah (i.e. from *bayt al mal)* the use of two bowls is permissible to the caliph. One to feed himself and his family and another to feed his people". [35]

Public and Private Interest

Drawing a clear line between public and private interests, Ali asks Malik Ashtar: [36]

1. Not to give land in permanent lease to relatives and

friends.

2. Sources of water supply should never be under the custody of private persons.
3. Lands, which have special public utility, should not be reserved for private use.

The reason cited by Ali was that if a privileged few "get possession of such holdings they will oppress others to derive undue benefits and thus gather all fruits for themselves leaving for you a bad reputation in this world and punishment in the next (world)". [37] It is apparent that Ali was afraid of concentration of wealth in a few hands and its subsequent socio-economic ill effects. Ali asks Malik Ashtar: "Do not reserve for yourself anything which is common property to all and in which others have equal rights". [38]

Abu Ubaid reports a narration similar to above. He narrates on the authority of Asbgah bin Banatah that he was with Ali when once the latter was taking a round of the market. Ali saw that a few traders had reserved certain places as their own. Disapproving the same Ali commented: "They do not have right to do so. The market place, to the Muslims, is like a mosque (where they cannot reserve a particular place for themselves). The market rule is that who so ever enters first, occupies a place for him till he himself leaves the place". [39]

In another narration in place of "mosque", the word "*eidgah*" has appeared. [40] This may be the case where markets do not have permanent structures. These may be daily or weekly markets for vegetables, fruits and flowers, etc. This may not apply in case where the markets have permanent structures and where shops, shelters are allotted on monthly or yearly rental basis. The point, which needs our consideration, is that in the opinion of Ali, none should claim or reserve a vacant public land for himself as a matter of right. Everyone should have an access to the public or common property resources.

Abu Muttar narrates that once Ali, holding a whip in his hand was taking a round of the market. [41] He addressed the traders in these words: "Sell but not under oaths. You may sell but there will be no blessings". Thereafter, after he inspected date sellers. There he saw a woman crying inconsolably. Ali enquired the reason. She informed him that she had purchased dates of a dirham for her master but the master rejected dates (may be because of poor quality). Ali asked the seller to take dates back as the maidservant had little control over it. The seller refused to oblige because he did not recognize Ali.

When he came to know that the man in question is Ali, he immediately took dates back and returned one dirham to the maidservant. He asked: "*Oh Ameerul Mumineen!* Are you displeased with me? Ali replied: "No I am not when you oblige your transactions". He made a common appeal to other sellers: "Feed the destitute, your earnings will multiply". [42] It is again clear that wherever may be Ali, poor and destitute are always in him mind. He must be thinking about their welfare.

Thereafter, Ali went to cloth merchants. He asked one merchant to sell one good quality shirt. The cloth merchant recognized him. Ali then refused to purchase the shirt. Ali went to another cloth merchant. He too recognized Ali and Ali refused to purchase. He went to another shop where a young boy was selling the shirts. He did not recognize Ali and Ali purchased a shirt in three dirham. While Ali was going back to his place, he saw a person running to him. He introduced himself as the father of young boy who sold shirt and wanted to return one dirham as the price of shirt was two dirham. Ali refused to accept it maintaining that the transaction was mutually consented and that no force was involved. [43] Ali did not like that someone should sell him a commodity at lower price or without profit simply because he was selling it to Ali, the caliph. In other words, Ali was against taking the undue advantage of position that he enjoyed.

Despise for Temporal Power

Ali, like other godly men and spiritual leaders, despises

temporal power and political office for being lowly and degrading. To him it is an instrument of gratification, of lust for power and political ambition. Ali looks down upon it with extreme contempt when the temporal power is desired as an end-in-itself and aspired as an ideal of life. He considers such kind of power devoid of any value and considers it more detestable than "a pig's bone in a leper's hand". However, Ali regards the same power as a matter of overriding importance when used as a means of establishing social justice.

Ali thought of the caliphate as a religious office and was of ascetic turn of mind with no ambitions save for his reward in heaven. During his period, Ali was very particular about his own conduct and that of his officers and their deputies. Had Ali ignored scrutiny of public in general and his lieutenants, in particular, masses would have been on his side, but Ali was a sharp scrutinizer, determined in carrying out his own ideas and unable to swerve from what his conscience dictated. Similar was the character of first two caliphs but their times were greatly different. There is no question of doubting the integrity and character of Usman too. The ground situation in his times was different.

However, Ali had to confront a very different situation. Under the changed circumstances, "Ali chalked out an ideal political policy from the first day of his caliphate. He could not have adopted any other course as some of his critics and historians suggest and plead that he could have, in that case, spared himself the hardships and difficulties he had to face in future". [44]

During the caliphate of Ali, the Byzantine emperor incited the protected people to revolt against the Muslim rule, which they refused. The refusal was mainly on account of religious policy of the cotemporary Byzantine Empire; if the emperor belonged to one sect, he did not tolerate other sects, still less other religions. The emperors were unpredictable and changed sects from time to time. The people had to follow suit by changing their sect and those who were unwilling to obey the emperor's orders were sentenced to have their noses or ears cut off.

They either were put to death or were subjected to all kinds of torture. "From one point of, remarks Bell, the triumph of Islam in the East in 7th Century A.D. may be regarded as the judgement of history upon a degenerate Christianity". [45] The Muslims on the other hand, allowed followers of other religions complete freedom, so much so that during the civil war, while Muslims were killing each other, the protected people lived in peace, engaged in trade and grew rich. Not much earlier, the conquest of Syria by Abu Bakr's army was a complete walkover and the "Christian population of the country welcomed the invaders as their liberators". [46]

The disturbed and turbulent period of Ali provided an ideal opportunity to the Byzantine ruler to get back their lost territories. Emperor Constantine II sent secretly a messenger to the Christians living in the Islamic state, exhorting them: "Here is the good opportunity: rise up against your government and I will also at the same time dispatch an army so that we may drive out this common enemy". The Christian population replied: "These enemies of our religion are preferable to you". The point was that they had never known anything like it even under their own Christian government. [47]

The above statement of the Christians brings to our notice two facts. First, the non-Muslim population enjoyed a great degree of freedom and protection under the Muslim rule. Secondly, it enables us to understand that the non-Muslim population had immense faith in the Muslim rule. Ali said: "Whosoever is our *zimmi,* (a protectorate) his blood is as sacred as our own and his property is as inviolable as our property". [48]

Had Ali become caliph in Umar's time, when the Muslims were still under the awe inspired by the Prophet and still zealous believers, he would probably have enjoyed a long and peaceful reign free from tension and internal squabbling; but when he become caliph, men's dispositions had already been spoiled, and political ambitions were ubiquitous. "It is reported that the Prophet said: 'When the family of so and so reaches thirty men, they take over Allah's property as (their personal) estates and reduce Allah's religion to corruption and make Allah's servants as their slaves". [49]

Ali alienated his own followers by his scrutiny of their conduct and his exactitude in religious matters. Many of his companions, therefore, abandoned his cause, including even his cousin Abdulla bin Abbas. Consequently, Muawiyah proceeded to win supporters by gifts and he gained control over a few followers of Ali by ruses. "Thus, the difference between Ali and Muawiyah were not confined to any particular issue which could have been solved by the ascendancy of one of the two contenders.

The issue in question was that there were two parallel standpoints and social orders each of which was comprehensive and antithesis of the other. And, we also maintain that if he (Ali) lacked craftiness, he did not suffer any great loss on account of it. Had he been more wily and astute, he would not have derived any benefit out of it, for the issue was whether the state should remain under the rightly guided caliphate or a monarchy". [50]

The reasons for civil strife, as noted by Ali, were the misuse of the power by the provincial governors and other high officers. He terminated services of all the governors and he made new appointments in their places. A change of action and reaction followed, which ultimately culminated in his martyrdom. He was martyred in the early morning of 24th January 661 C.E. while inviting the people taking rest in the mosque to get ready for morning prayers. [51] As a martyr, he retrieved more than what he had lost in his lifetime. His eldest son, Hasan, remarked: "Oh people! Last night a person departed from us. Neither the predecessors nor the successors will have an edge over him. He left behind neither gold nor silver. Out of his allowances, he had saved 700 hundred dirham to purchase a slave, which alas he could not purchase". [52] His entire lifetime and mission may be summed up as a case where while the value-based system was collapsing, Ali succeeded astoundingly.

End Notes

1. *Kanzul Umaal:* Narration No. 14315.
2. *Nahjul Balagha,* p. 150.
3. *Nahjul Balagha,* p. 151.
4. Ibid.
5. *Kanzul Umaal:* Narration No. 14286.
6. *Kanzul Umaal:* Narration No. 14366.
7. *Nahjul Balagha*, p. 144.
8. *Kanzul Ummal:* Narration No. 17049.
9. Nadvi, S.A.A., *The Life of Caliph Ali,* op. cit., p. 187.
10. *Nahjul Balagha,* Sermon No. 221.
11. Ibid.
12. *Kitab al-Amwal:* Narration No. 11.
13. *Nahjul Balagha,* Sermon No. 221.
14. *Nahjul Balagha,* Sermon No. 221.
15. Ibid.
16. There is also a tradition of the Prophet, which highlights this, along with many others, as the clear sign of the fast approaching doom's day.
17. The appellation of "Al-Ashtar" is Arabic meaning cut, torn or ripped. He earned the title of "Al-Ashtar" from a battle scar he received on his lower eyelid in the Battle of Yarmouk (636 C.E.) during the caliphate of Umar.
18. Anthaki, Abdul Maseeh, quoted in the English translation of *Nahjul Balagha*, pp. 492-493.
19. Ibid. The Shia, in addition to the Constitution of Medina, refer to this particular letter of Ali wherein principles of government were set. Please refer to Werner Ende and Udo Steinbach (eds.), *Islam in the World Today,* Cornell University Press, Cornell, 2010, p. 198.
20. Ibid.
21. *Nahjul Balagha*, p. 494.
22. *Musnad Abi Awaana:* Vol. I.
23. Ibid.
24. *Nahjul Balagha,* Letter No. 5.

25. Ibid.
26. *Nahjul Balagha,* Letter No. 46.
27. *Nahjul Balagha*, pp. 496-497.
28. *Nahjul Balagha*, p. 498.
29. Ibid.
30. Ibid.
31. *Nahjul Balagha*, p. 500.
32. Ibid and also S.A.A. Moududi, *Khilafat wa Malukiat,* op. cit., p. 78.
33. *Nahjul Balagha*, p. 495.
34. *Nahjul Balagha*, p. 507.
35. *Kanzul Umaal:* Narration Nos. 14348-14349.
36. *Nahjul Balagha*, p. 508.
37. Ibid.
38. *Nahjul Balagha*, p. 510.
39. *Kitab al-Amwal:* Narration No. 226.
40. *Kanzul ummal:* Narration No. 16840. "Eidgah" is a place where annual congregational prayers are offered. It is normally situated outside the city limits.
41. From this narration one can gauge the importance market supervision and regulation.
42. *KanzulUummal:* Narration No. 36547.
43. Ibid.
44. Al-Aqqad, Abbas Mahmud, *Al-Abqariyat al Islamiyah,* quoted by Sayed Abul Hasan Ali Nadwi, *The Life of Caliph Ali,* op. cit., p. 189.
45. Nizami, Khaliq Ahmad, *Some Aspects of Religion and Politics During the Thirteenth Century*, op. cit., p. 11.
46. Hamidullah, Muhammad, "Tolerance in the Prophet's Deeds at Madinah", op. cit.
47. Ibid.
48. Hussain, Shaik Shoukat, *Human Rights in Islam*, op. cit., p. 59. See also *Hazart Ali Murtuda* by Masudul Hasan, Aakif Book Depot, Delhi; Syed Abul Hasan Ali Nadvi, *The Life of Caliph Ali,* op. cit.
49. Al-Daudi, *Kitab al Kharuj,* op. cit., p. 73.
50. Al-Aqqad, op. cit., pp. 189-190.
51. Ibne Muljim, the assassin, was brought before a fatally wounded Ali with his hands tied to his back. Ali saw that the rope with which he was tied was cutting into his flesh. He forgot his own

wounds, felt that though Ibne Muljim had delivered a fatal blow yet he was a human being, and should be treated as such. He ordered to loosen the bonds of Ibne Muljim and to treat him humanly. The kindness touched the heart of assassin and he started weeping, so did everybody. A smile appeared on Ali's face and in a faint voice he said: "It is too late to repent now, you have done your deed, was I a bad Imam, Ibne Muljim? For further details please refer to *Nahjual Balagha*, p. 274.

52. *Kanzul Ummal:* Narration No. 36574.

8

Essence of Alinomics

Introduction

A systematically dispassionate study of the economic ideas of Ali makes it clear that he was a distinct precursor to several economic values, which even today, continue to dominate the main stream economic thinking. He excelled in both letter and spirit, whenever a new economic problem or issue came before him. The justification, which Ali provided on several economic issues, was amazingly incredible and never heard before.

The need for a systematic study arises in order to understand the essence of economic ideas of Ali. Not much is written on various aspects of Ali's multidimensional accomplishments and not much literature is available to highlight the sincere cooperation, which Ali extended to his predecessors as their advisor. There is a need to analyze dispassionately the critically complex situation prevailing during his brief period of caliphate (656-661 C.E.) that came in the way of effective implementation of his economic ideas. He had to face instability, divisions, conflict of socio-economic interests, which his predecessors did not.

As far as writings on the history of Islamic economic thought are concerned, highest numbers of publications are on Ibn Khaldun, Ibn Taimiyyah and Abu Yusuf. There is no major work devoted exclusively to the study of economic ideas of Ali in a systematic and methodological way. Several passing references are made to his ideas, sayings and actions but these remain scattered. Ali's moral, spiritual and juristic contributions have over shadowed his economic ideas, principles and administration. Several authors, writing on the life and times of Ali, have not paid adequate attention to a study of his economics ideas.

There are several celebrated aspects of Ali's personality. He never gave up the companionship of Abu Bakr. He never absented himself from the congregational prayers led by Abu Bakr. At that particular time, Ali made it clear that the interest of Islam and the newly formed Islamic state was above all. He was free from clannish bias; he had no hidden political agenda; he would do nothing to cause divisions in the community and that he was sincere and honest to the core. The later events also proved that he was honest to the core. His devotion to the cause of Islam was matchless.

The second caliph Umar used to seek Ali's counsel in important matters. When the life of Usman, the third caliph, was under threat, Ali not only advised him sincerely but also provided physical protection. Ali asked his sons, Hasan and Hussain, to guard Usman's residence. Ali also the commoners, as and when they approached him with their religious and juristic problems.

During the period of Umar, conquests, far and wide, had brought in immense wealth and prosperity, changing the way of life of the people. Islam was getting globalised so also the social structure of people. When Usman embraced Islam, things were different and when he became caliph situation had undergone a major change. The class composition of the society changed so fast that it was becoming increasingly difficult to reconcile different competing interests.

Umar was a strong man and ruled with an iron hand. He rigorously imposed the Islamic morality. He meted out severe punishments to the offenders to check the corrupt practices and could dismiss many influential officers from their postings without any opposition. He succeeded mainly because there was not available any asylum to offenders and there was no alternative power centre, as we find during the reign of Ali. After the assassination of Usman, people thronged around Ali urging him to accept the leadership of Muslims. There was no caliph for three days and complete disorder and bewilderment prevailed. Such a situation did not exist when Abu Bakr, Umar and Usman became caliphs. There were no dissenters either.

By the time Ali became caliph, the egalitarian structure of the Arabian society had been nearly shattered. Muslim society got itself divided into various groups. Ali wanted to shape his policies in accordance with the teachings of Islam, especially its egalitarian spirit by enforcing Islamic laws rigorously. Ali found it extremely difficult to execute his policies and he too ultimately fell prey to the sword of an assassin. In a decisive historical struggle, Ali lost and his adversaries won, heralding an era of *mulukiat* (dynastic rule). With the establishment of Umayyad dynasty, the golden age of the Prophet and the Rightly Guided Caliphs ended and the caliphate became an absolute monarchy.

Essence of Personal Approach of Ali

The personal approach has a great bearing upon the way in which a person conducts himself, publicly as well as privately and how he manages affairs individually as well as collectively. In Ali, we do not find any trait of revenge. Long before he became caliph, Ali had defeated a powerful foe in the battle. He was just about to kill him, the latter spat on his face. Ali immediately got off his chest and let him go.

Ali was an epitome of magnanimity. In the battle of Siffin (657 C.E.), Ali recaptured river Euphrates from Muawiyah. Earlier, Muawiyah and his army did not allow Ali's army to take water from the river when it was under their control. It was now Muawiyah's turn to beseech permission to get water, which Ali readily granted despite opposition from his own soldiers.

Ali stood for truth and justice. He never had any personal interest. In the battle of Nahrwan, (657 C.E.) Ali was fighting like any other ordinary soldier. A soldier from the rival party came to fight against Ali, and in the encounter, he lost his sword. When asked, Ali gave his sword. The soldier realising the greatness of Ali requested him to fight from Ali's side. Ali replied: "Friend fight for the truth and justice and do not fight for persons".

Ali preferred peace to war and even during wartime never attacked first. He respected covenants. Whenever Ali sent soldiers on expeditions, he urged them to deal gently with the enemy, and particularly to see that no harm befell the women. Before the Battle of Jamal actually began, for three days, Ali invited his adversaries for a dialogue and compromise. Ali instructed his soldiers: "Do not chase when a soldier (after being defeated) is running away; do not kill a wounded soldier; peace and security to those who keep their doors closed; peace and security to those who surrender; their wealth will not be treated as *ghanimah*; women's honour will be protected; children will not be imprisoned".

Ali held human blood as highly sacred. While assuming the burden of caliphate, Ali highlighted the sacredness of human blood. On his deathbed, he remained particular about it. Ali, despite great pressure on him, remained uncompromising and fought alone, for principles, until he was assassinated.

Ali was so magnanimous that he recognized the rights of *kharijites* who were his bitter opponents. They were not prevented them from offering prayers in the mosques; they were allowed a share in *fai'* and no war was not declared against them until they attacked. Abu Ubaid comments that Ali approved *kharijites'* share in *fai* even though they used filthy language against Ali. They continued to create problems and made things difficult for Ali.

The only characteristic, which Ali lacked, was opportunism and unscrupulousness. His failures, if there were, can be attributed to this and to the fear of God and love for Islam, which often withheld him from taking a wrong, hasty, partial and short-sighted stand. He was a fervent Muslim, honest in both speech and action, unacquainted with crooked ways and tricks. His sole concern was religion and the basis of all his actions was the truth.

Ali conducted himself above the narrow considerations of

clan, class and colour. He never showed preference to his relatives. Nepotism was not there. Ali practiced ascetism and led a life of detachment from worldly comforts. When some friends found him shivering in the cold they advised him to get a woollen blanket from the *bayt-al-maal* but he choose to forgo it. Colleagues impressed upon Ali that he and his family members have their right over *bayt al maal.* Ali refused their advice maintaining that he did want to put pressure upon *bayt al maal.*

On an occasion while marching toward Basra, Ali along with Abdullah ibn Abbas stopped at Ziquar. Abdullah ibn Abbas found Ali putting stitches to and repairing his very old worn out shoes. Ali asked ibn Abbas: "What do you think would be the cost of this pair of shoes? He replied: "Nothing Sir! Not even the cost of stitches put on them. They are worthless". Ali replied: "Ibn Abbas if I cannot establish a regime of justice and truth and if cannot eradicate tyranny and impiety, then the value of this caliphate is less to me than the cost of this pair of shoes".

When compared with Abu Dhar Ghiffari, Ali was not that an extremist but was against concentration of wealth in a few hands. Ali favoured neither ostentatious living nor the life of a hermit. In case of commoners, he favoured moderation and for the men of affairs his advice was to practice extreme simplicity.

Ali did not exhibit any favouritism, not even to his relatives, including his son Hasan. Someone asked Ali, on his deathbed, whether he would like to appoint someone as his successor, he replied: "No! I leave you as the Prophet had left you". All the four rightly guided caliphs had worthy sons who deserved caliphate, had it ever been entrusted to them. However, none of them did so out of the fear of Allah and due to compassion for others.

Essence of Economic Ideas of Ali

By the time Ali became caliph, socio-economic conditions

had changed drastically. Internal troubles did not allow him to concentrate much on economic and financial affairs. During the caliphate of Abu Bakr and Umar, Ali made a few assertions. These, to some extent, help us to visualize his economic vision. When Ali himself became the caliph, the internal strife and bloodshed made things difficult. He, therefore, did not get sufficient time to implement his economic vision over which he was thinking before assuming caliphate. In this context, the essence of Ali's economic vision should be studied with reference to the mobilization and distribution of public resources. These two were his prime peacetime concerns.

In Ali's ideas, we find a fine convergence of ability-to-pay and benefit principles of taxation. Conventionally, in the payment of taxes there is no *quid pro quo*. Ali, however, tagged payment of taxes to the benefits received. In Ali's vision, there is no question of payment when benefits are not received. Once, a person approached Ali with his *zakah* dues. Ali asked him: "Do you receive any stipend or monetary assistance from *bayt al maal*". He replied in negative. Ali then asked him to go back maintaining that the government will not collect anything from him. "We do not want to overburden you. We do not want to trouble you. The first trouble is that you are not paid anything from *bayt al maal.* Secondly, we should not trouble you by collecting *zakah*". At the same time Ali asked his tax officers to consider the productivity of land and tax bearing capacity of people, thus, clearing incorporating the ability-to-pay ideal.

Land taxation continued to remain an important fiscal issue in Ali's reign too. He made necessary changes with regard to the categories of land and rates of land tax. Ali introduced an element of progression: the rate of *kharaj* increasing from 0.5 dirham to 1.5 dirham depending upon the type of land. When we consider land as a taxable asset, the fiscal message of Ali is that even productive assets, including land, can be taxed at progressive rates and different slabs can be introduced. Currently, progressive taxation of income is exercised in respect of persons only while corporate companies are taxed at a flat rate. This make burden of tax to fall on persons and not on corporate.

It is also clear from Ali's tax policy that the tax rate in case of specific items/assets could be high when the yield/return from them is high. For example, as compared to a levy of 1.5 dirham on most fertile land (Grade I), he collected 10 dirham (nearly seven-eight times more) from the farmers cultivating vine and palms groves. Further, during his caliphate Ali, for the purpose of *jiziyah,* put non-Muslims protectorates into different categories, depending upon ownership of wealth.

Here also Ali introduced an element of progression, well-off *ahlul z-zimmah* paying more *jiziyah*. The basis of charge was their wealth. Currently, the wealth tax is considered as a minor direct tax. It covers less number of taxpayers and its contribution to the total tax revenue collection is also less. In the context of growing income consumption inequalities, the progressive taxation of wealth is surely a matter of serious consideration. Ali's practices, if adopted and extended to other productive and remunerative assets, may revolutionize taxation of wealth.

In the matters of taxation, the overall approach of Ali contains "supply-side" ideals. This refers to a policy wherein importance is attached to production and productive agents. It may be recalled here that Ali wrote a letter to one of his governors to keep in view the welfare of taxpayers, which is of primary importance that the taxes themselves. He held the view that the taxpayers are the original sources of revenue on which the welfare of the state and its subjects depended.

Ali asked his officers to attach more importance to the fertility of land than to the collection of taxes because actual taxable capacity of people rests upon the fertility of the land. Ali believed that a head of state who does not pay attention to the prosperity of his subjects and fertility of land but concentrates only the collection of revenue, lays waste the land, ruins the state and brings destruction to the creatures of God. His rule cannot last for long.

Ali was against 'heavy burden of taxation', on persons and their properties. He asked his officers to reduce taxpayers' burden as and when the situation warranted. Ali believed that the prosperity of cities and their people greatly depend upon a humane tax policy. A just tax policy, Ali opined, not only nets more revenue but it earns respect and command of people. In a prosperous country, people willing come forward to clear their tax dues.

Ali incorporated a human element in tax administration when, elsewhere, taxes were known as notorious means of exploitation and subjugation. Ali knew it very well that the governments elsewhere were unpopular among their peoples mainly because of the force used in tax collection. In one of the letters, Ali wrote: "Do not let the Muslims grieve (over their lot of having you as their ruler) and do not approach them in a way as to make your approach hateful to them. Do not tax them more than what is actually due from them to Allah".

Ali held the view that the abject and wretched living of people was because of the desire of rulers and officers to amass huge wealth. He remarked that 'they never learnt any lesson from the history of nations and never paid any attention to the orders of God'. In this context, Ali's instructions are worth studying as humane, face of his tax administration emerges. Ali wrote to the *kharaj* collectors forbidding them to lay hands on the cultivators' clothes, both summer and winter, articles of their daily use, farm animals and their household objects. To another officer, Ali advised that he should not flog anyone, sell his provisions, his winter or summer garments. *Kharaj*payers should not be pressurized to sell their animals and seasonal clothing to clear their dues.

The economy of early Islamic state was quite rudimentary hence, there was no sophisticated mechanism of resource distribution. It is, however, to the credit of Islam that it rearranged the distributive role of the budget wherein the financing of requirements of poor and destitute received top priority. Never before Islam, was an institutionalized effort made to ameliorate the economic position of poor and destitute. During the period of Prophet, the contours of distribution policy had started emerging. In the beginning, the Prophet provided financial assistance to the needy and poor on an *adhoc* basis. When revenue started multiplying, the whole distribution process was regularized.

In the area of distribution too, Ali has left his clear imprints. In the context of distribution of annexed land, one instance can be cited from the period of Umar. Ali impressed upon the Caliph 'to leave the land to its cultivators. If land is distributed amongst army personnel it will remain consolidated in some hands forever'. Ali suggested that the lands be made a source of income for Muslims and thus be immobilized. Otherwise, according to Ali 'it would create landlordism in Islam'. Ali was afraid of Muslims becoming overbearing and insolent landlords. Caliph Umar also thought that once Muslims become landlords, they would start fighting for rights over waters.

Ali was against disturbing the then existing occupancy of cultivators. Any displacement would have led to mass unemployment and loss of income. Mass out migration would have also taken place mainly to certain urban centres. What Ali thought was that, as a matter of public policy, the interest of commoners should be preferred to the material gain of army personnel.

Following doubtlessly the example set by the Prophet, Abu Bakr divided the state revenue among Muslims. Every Muslim received his share, which depended upon familial requirements. True, in the beginning it was very meagre but went on increasing in the following years. No difference was made between those who accepted Islam before or after the conquest of Makkah.

Umar (634-644 C.E.) changed the policy of equal distribution. He showed preference to those who had accepted

Islam prior to the conquest of Makkah. After a few years, Umar realised the concentration of wealth and concomitant imbalances in the socio-economic structure of the early Islamic society. He wanted to change the policy of unequal distribution. His martyrdom, however, came in the way of accomplishing that particular task.

During the caliphate of Usman (644-656 C.E.), the policy of restraining Muslims from acquiring or owning landed property in conquered countries was given up. He took another decision of far reaching economic consequences. In order to induce Hejazis, settled at Kufa, to go back to the Hejaz and to reduce pressure of population in Kufa, he permitted them to exchange their lands held in Iraq with those in Hejaz.

Many took advantage of this opportunity, exchanged their barren land in Hejaz for the most fertile land in other provinces, and in no time became big holders. Thus, came into existence in an Islamic society a class of big landlords.

The purpose, for which Usman had initiated these measures, i.e., easing the pressure of population in the conquered provinces, remained fulfilled.

On the contrary, two classes emerged namely the landlords and the landless, mainly slaves. The big landlords and their landholdings created demand for more slave labour.

Ali changed the course of this policy of distribution. Ali's policy of abstinence and detachment, did not allow him to see the inequalities growing. His impartial stand, did not allow anyone, including his brothers, relatives and officers to lead a life of extravagance at the cost of mass poverty.

When Ali took the charge of caliphate, he found that large fiefs and estates were granted to certain persons. Well-wishers of Ali advised him to overlook and ignore previous distribution. He, however, handed back all the fiefs and estates to the public treasury.

Immediately after becoming the caliph, Ali started reforming, reorganizing the management of public treasury in general, and accounts department in particular. He removed dishonest officers from services. Ali reorganized the *zakah* based expenditure policy reflecting the essence of Quranic classification [9:60]. During the caliphate of Ali, revenue from *jiziyah* and *kharaj* was earmarked for the maintenance of army; construction and maintenance of forts; construction and maintenance of roads and bridges; maintenance and repairs of wells and construction of rest houses.

Since masses were poor, Ali adopted a system of weekly distribution of public funds. On every Thursday, funds were distributed so that Muslims could happily spend their weekly holiday on Friday. Every Thursday, accounts were closed and every Saturday started with fresh books of accounts. After the distribution was over and accounts cleared, Ali used to sweep and clean entire building of *bayt al maal*. He used to offer prayers in the Treasury itself, thanking his Lord that he had performed his duty faithfully. Ali should be, therefore, considered as a precursor of 'zero-based budgeting'.

Ali had a very clear perception of *bayt al maal*. He treated public money as one the forms of trust, the other being governance. Once one of his close companions by name Abdullah bin Zumma requested for some money from the public treasury. Ali refused and replied: "The public treasury is neither my property nor yours. It is the property of Muslims, either it is collected through their exertions (when they pay *zakah* out of their wealth, etc.) or it is booty of their wars". This statement once again clarifies Ali's perception of *bayt al maal* that the wealth deposited with *bayt al maal* is public property and no one, not even caliph, has any special claim over it.

Ali drew a clear line between public and private interests. He prohibited his governors from giving land in permanent lease to their relatives and friends. "Sources of water supply should never be under the custody of private persons. Lands, which have special public utility, should not be reserved for private use". He compared open market places as the mosques where no one has a place reserved oneself.

In the interest of a sound public administration, Ali believed in continuity. He did not change certain policy decisions of his predecessors even though, after becoming caliph, he had a chance. When Ali made Kufa as the seat of caliphate, he declared it publicly: "I have not come here to cancel and reverse decisions made and implemented by Umar". Another remark is attributed to Ali: "I have not come here to untie what has been already firmly tied down by Umar". Imam al-Baqir is quoted to have said, "Ali followed Abu Bakr and Umar. By God! Ali did not like that he should be blamed for opposing Abu Bakr and Umar.

Essence of Ali's Ideas on Governance

Ali's vision of governance is clear from his very first public sermon as the caliph. "Fear God in fulfilling your obligations to the creatures of God and their habitations. You will be questioned about the beasts and the land (on the Day of Judgement). I ask you again to obey Allah and keep away from His disobedience and sins. Adopt if you find anything virtuous; shun if you find evil".

In one of the sermons, Ali, as the caliph, remarked: "It is a duty of the ruler of the Muslims to rule according to the law of Almighty and be truthful to them. While he is doing so, it is a duty of the subjects to obey and to listen to him. They should respond to his call whenever such a call is made". In letter and spirit, the first sermon of Ali is very much similar to those of Abu Bakr and Umar. Ali stressed the need for a powerful and benevolent government. He battled against the views propagated by the *khawarij* (secedors).

According to Ali, the mission of caliphate is achieved only when: (a) a regime of justice and truth is established, and (b) tyranny and impiety are checked.

Ali provided much needed socio-economic space to the poor. He is reported to have remarked: "I am thankful to Allah for having selected me (as the caliph) for this service (to the poor). Further, attending to the needs of poor and destitute is more valuable to me than the entire deposits of gold and silver on this earth".

During the regime of Ali, the poor always found a prime position, be it in his religious sermons, official instructions, letters, and public pronouncements. Notwithstanding the numerous civil wars, the poorest and downtrodden from amongst Muslims in general and "protected peoples" in particular, felt greatly safe and secured. Ali sympathised with the poor and downtrodden for the reason that, except a few, almost every prophet was raised from amongst poor. When he himself became the caliph, he favoured a life of poverty to affluence. He led a life characterized by the real traits of poverty. According to Ali these traits were "faces pinched with famine, dry with thirst and blear-eyed with tears".

Ali wanted that his government should be pro-poor and it should sensitize issues relating to the poverty and sufferings of masses. He instructed his governors that: "*When poor cannot reach you, you must reach the poor.* This pro-poor role of the government was advocated and practiced at a time when poor and deprived were left at the mercy of nature to fend for themselves. They never found any place in public agenda. In the present day secular economies, it is a very recent phenomenon that the governments have started responding to the needs of poor and vulnerable sections.

In respect of poor, deprived and disabled persons, Ali wrote to his governors that "it is *absolutely* necessary that they should be looked after, helped and well provided for". Ali identified himself with poor and weak. He used to remark: "Shall I be content and satisfied simply because people call me *Amir-ul-Momineen* (commander of faithful)? Shall I not sympathize with the faithful Muslims in their calamities, shall I not be their partner in their adversities, shall I not be their fellow in suffering? Shall I not set an example for them to patiently, courageously, bravely and virtuously bear up hardships and bereavements?

Ali refused sumptuous and delicious food maintaining, "I

want to eat the kind of food which the poorest of my realm can afford at least once a day. I shall improve it after I have improved their standard of life. I want to live, feel and suffer like them". He believed that attending to the needs of poor and destitute was more valuable to him than the entire deposits of gold and silver on this earth.

Ali was very particular about the conduct of his officers with regard to the poor and downtrodden. Someone invited Usman bin Hunaif, one of the trusted companions of Ali and the governor of Basra province, for dinner. When Ali came to know of this, he immediately wrote a letter expressing his displeasure in clear words. "I am sorry to hear the news. I never expected that you would accept invitation of persons who invites high officers and rich people and from whose door poor persons and hungry paupers are turned away rudely".

Ali did not compromise with the principles and, even in the most trying situations, stood for principles. While being caliph, Ali had had two options. The first one was to tread the path of equity and justice at the cost of his own life, power and caliphate. The second alternative was to sacrifice the principles of equity and justice and thereby strengthen his position and save his rule. These two indeed were competing options. Ali, as was expected from an upright person and a noble soul, favoured the policy of equity and justice at the cost of his rule and life.

Appendices

Appendix 1

Important Dates (Christian Era)

Year	Event
599/600	Birth of Ali.
605	Ali becomes the ward of the Prophet.
610	Public pronouncement of Islam.
615	A batch of Muslims migrate to Abyssinia under the leadership of Jafar, the elder brother of Ali.
617	The Hashimites are ex-communicated by the Quraiash.
619	Year of Sorrow, death of Abu Talib, Ali's father and Khadija, the wife of the Prophet.
620	The ascension of the Prophet.
622	The Prophet migrates to Madinah. Ali risks his life for the sake of Prophet by sleeps on the bed of the Prophet on the night of migration. The opponents had planned to attack the Prophet.
623	Ali migrates and settles at Madinah, helps in the construction of *Masjidun Nabi* (the Prophet's mosque).
624	Battle of Badr; operations against the Jews of Bani Qainuqa; marriage of Ali with Fatima, the daughter of the Prophet.
625	Battle of Uhud; operations against the Jews of the Banu Nadir; birth of eldest son Hasan.

627	Battle of Trench; operations against Banu Quraiza, Banu Mustaliq and Banu Saad.
628	Pilgrimage to Makkah; the Hudaibiyah pact; the conquest of Khyber.
631	Mubahala with the Christians of Najran; expedition against Banu Rumla; Operation against Banu Zubuda; Ali's mission to Yemen.
632	The Farewell Pilgrimage; The Prophet delivers sermon at Khum Ghadir; the Prophet passes away; Abu Bakr declared as the caliph.
633	Death of Fatima, Ali's wife.
634	Death of Abu Bakr; Nomination of Umar as the Caliph.
644	Death of Umar; Election of Usman as the Caliph.
656	Martyrdom of Usman, Election of Ali as the Caliph; Rebellion of Talha, Zubair, Ayesha, Battle of Jamal.
657	Shifting of capital to Kufah; Battle of Siffin.
658	The Arbitration, the Battle of Nahrawan.
659	Muawiyah's occupation of Egypt; Trouble in Basra; Raids of Muawiyah.
660	Muawiyah declares himself as the caliph at Damascus.
661	Martyrdom of Ali; eldest son Hasan elected as Caliph; after six months Hasan steps down.

Appendix 2

Select Glossary of Islamic Terms

Term	Meaning
Ahul z-Zimmah	Non-Muslim subjects of an Islamic state who pay poll tax and enjoy security of their lives and properties.
Al-adl	Equilibrium.
Adalah	Justice.
Al-ahsan	Compassion.
Amir	A ruler, a commander, a chief, a leader, a nobleman.
Amir ul mumineen	Commander of faithful.
Al-anfal	Spoils. It is the title of Surah VIII of the Quran in which are given directions regarding the division of the spoils of war.
Ashab	Pl. of sahib. The companions of the Prophet. The accepted view is that one who embraced Islam, saw the Prophet and sat in his company even for a short time is a sahabi.
Bai'	Sale, commercial dealings, barter.
Bait ul Maal	Lit. The house of property. The public treasury of an Islamic state, which the ruler is not allowed to use for his personal expenses but only for public good. The revenue sources, among others, are zakah , khums, the produce of mines and treasure

	trove, property of which there is no owner and jiziyah.
Daru' l-Islam	Land of Islam. It is a country in which the edicts of Islam are fully promulgated.
Dhimmi	Protectorate, ahl u-zimmah.
Din	Religion, life of piety.
Dinar	A gold coin.
Dirham	A silver coin.
Diwan	Accounts book, muster rolls, register.
Dunya	World.
Fai	It is booty taken from a country which submits to Islam without resistance.
Faqih	A Muslim theologian.
Farz	Obligatory.
Fatwa	A religious decree pronounced by a mufti or qazi.
Fiqh	The dogmatic theology of Muslims.
Ghanimah	Wealth obtained during the course of war. Four-fifth belongs to the troops and remaining one-fifth must be divided into three equal portions for the relief of orphans, the feeding of poor and entertainment of travellers.
Hadis Qudsi	A divine saying, a term used for a hadith which relates to the revelation from God in the language of the Prophet.
Halal	Lawful, permissible.
Hanafi	A school of fiqh named after Imam-e-

	Azam Abu Hanifa. The Imam was born in Kufa in 80 A.H. He was a great oracle of jurisprudence and with his two pupils, Imam Abu Yusuf and Imam Muhammad, founded Hanafi School.
Hanbali	A school of fiqh named after Imam Ahmad bin Hanbal. He was born in Baghdad in 164 A.H.
Haram	Prohibited, unlawful.
Hijaz	It is tract of land which separates Najd from Tahmah and is an irregular parallelogram about 250 miles long and 150 miles wide. It is considered as the holy land and the two sacred cities of Makkah and Madina are within its limits.
Hijr	In its primitive sense it means interdiction or prevention.
Hijrah	Lit. Migration. Islamic calendar year commences with the hijrah which marks the migration of the Prophet from Makkah to Madina in 622 C.E.
Himah	Lit. Guarded, forbidden. A portion of land reserved as grazing ground for animals.
Hudaibiya	It is a well on an open space on the verge of Haram (sacred territory), which encircles Makkah. Celebrated as the place of truce between the Prophet and the people of Quraish and other clans.
Ihitikar	Hoarding the grain with the object of raising the price.
Ilm	Knowledge. Hence, aalim (scholar) and ulema (scholars).

Ijma	Unanimous consent of learned scholars.
Ijtihad	The logical deduction on a legal or theological question by a mujtahid (a learned scholar).
Iman	Faith, belief.
Infaq	Spending, giving forth.
Iqtisad	Moderation.
Islam	Submission to the Will of Allah.
Israf	Waste.
Jahiliya	Age of ignorance.
Jareeb	A jareed is equal to 60 yards.
Jihad	Striving, struggle, effort.
Jizyah	Poll tax imposed upon non-Muslim citizens of an Islamic state.
Kafir	One who denies or hides truth.
Kanz	Treasure, especially gold and silver buried in the ground.
Kharaj	A tribute, tax on land.
Khalifa	Caliph.
Khwarij	Pl. of khariji. Heretics, schimatics. Especially those who rebelled against Ali.
Khulfa'u r Rashidun	The well directed caliphs. The first four successor of the Prophet namely Abu Bakr (632-634), Umar (634-644), Usman (644-656) and Ali (656-661). After the martyrdom of Ali, the Banu Umaiyah succeeded in founding Ummaid dynasty (661-749).

Khums	A fifth of the property which given to the baitul maal.
Luqtah	Troves.
Maal	Wealth, property.
Maliki	A school of fiqh founded by Imam Malik. He was born at Madinah in 95 A.H.
Miskin	Needy person.
Mu'akhat	Brotherhood, fraternization.
Mufti	The officer who expounds the law.
Muhajir	Migrant.
Muhtakir	A forestaller. One who monopolizes grain and other necessities of life to create an artificial shortage.
Muhtasib	A public sensor of religion and morals.
Mulhid	One who has deviated from the truth.
Munafiq	A hypocrite.
Muslim	One who submits to the Will of Allah.
Nisab	A certain size of property or wealth at which the zakah becomes due.
Qazi	A judge.
Qiyas	Analogical reasoning of the learned men.
Riba	Usury.
Rikaz	Treasure buried in the earth.
Sa'	A certain measure of grain.
Sabilu'llah	Road of God. A term used for any good act to please Allah.

Sadqah	Alms giving.
Sahibu'nisab	A person who owns a certain minimum size of property or wealth on which zakah becomes due.
Shafi'i	A school of fiqh founded by Imam Muhammad bin Idris as-Shafi'i. He was born at Asqlan, in Palestine in 150 A.H.
Shariah	The law including both the dictates of the Quran and the traditions of the Prophet.
Shia	The partisans. Popularly, the term is used for persons who favoured that Ali should succeed the Prophet.
Silsila	Chain, link. Sufi order. Pl. Salasil.
Sufi	Mystic, purified. A person who has overpowered his evil self. Pl. Sufiya
Sunnah	A path or way, a manner of life. Popularly, the traditions of the Prophet which record either the saying and doings of the Prophet.
Taba'i	One who sat in the company of the Companions of the Prophet. Pl. Tabi'un.
Tafsir	Lit. Explaining, a term commonly used for commentary on the Quran.
Tauhid	Unity of God.
Tijarah	Commerce, merchandise.
Ummah	Islamic community.
Ushr	A tenth or tithe.
Ushur	Octroi.

Waqf	Endowment.
Wasaq	A camel load.
Zakah	Lit. Purification. A levy on eligible Muslims. One of the five fundamental tenets of Islam.
zuhd	Asceticism; not setting ones heart on worldly things.
zuhud wa war'ah	Abstinence and temperance. Temperance involves giving up the love of worldly things for the love of God. Abstinence involves purifying the heart and mind from the defilement and pollutants of the world.

Bibliography

Bibliography

Abu Jafar Ahmad ibn Nasr al-Daudi, *Kitab al-Amwal,* Islamic Research Institute, Islamabad, Pakistan, 1995.

Abul Hassan Syed Mohammed Razi, *Nahjul Balagha.* It is rendered into English by Askari Jafery and entitled as *Peak of Eloquence*, published by Islamic Seminary, Bombay, 1978.

Abu Ubaid Al Qasim bin Sallam, *Kitab al-Amwal,* Idarah-e-Tahqiqat-e-Islami, Islamabad, Pakistan, 1986.

Abu Yusuf, *Kitab al Kharaj,* Al-Matabtal Salfia, Egypt, 2nd Edition, 1352.

Aghnides, *Muhammadan Theories of Finance,* Idarah-i-Adbiyat-e-Dilli, Delhi,

Ameer Ali, Syed, *The Spirit of Islam*, Kitab Bhavan, 1997.

Amini, Muhammad Taqi, *Agrarian System of Islam*, Idarah-i-Adbiyat-e-Dilli, Delhi, 1991.

Atta Mohy-ud-din's, *Abu Bakr,* S. Chand & Co., New Delhi, 1968.

Ausaf Ahmad and Abdul Azeem Islahi, (eds.) *Economic Problems and the Teaching of the Quran,* Idarah Uloom al-Quran, Aligarh, 2011.

Bailey, Stephen J. *Strategic Public Finance*, Palgrave MacMillan, 2004.

Baksh, Khuda, *Politics in Islam,* Idarah-i Adabiyat-i Delli, first published in 1920 and reprinted in 1981. It is an English translation of Von Kremer's *Staadsidee des Islam,* originally published in German.

Chirri, Muhammad Jawad, *The Brother of Prophet Mohammad*, Ansariyan Publications, Qum, Iran, (in two volumes), 1996.

Engineer, Asghar Ali, *The Origins and Development of Islam,* Ikraq Publications, Kuala Lumpur, 1980.

Engineer, Asghar Ali, *The Islamic State*, Vikas Publishing House Pvt. Ltd., New Delhi, 1994.

Engineer, Asghar Ali, *On Developing Theology of Peace in Islam,* Sterling Publishers Pvt. Ltd., New Delhi, 2003.

Esposito, John L., *Islam: The Straight Path,* Oxford University Press, 1998.

Fuller, Graham E., *A World Without Islam*, Little Brown Company, London, 2010.

Gulen, Fetthullah M., *The Inifite Light: An Analysis of the Life of the Prophet Muhammad,* Adam Publishers and Distributors, New Delhi, 2012.

Haque, Ziaul, *Landlord and Peasant in Early Islam,* Islamic Research Institute, Islamabad, 1984.

Hasan uz Zaman S.M., *The Economic Functions of the Early Islamic State.*

Haykal, Muhammad Husayn, *Siddiq-e-Akbar* (Urdu), 2nd Edition, Islamic Book Foundation, New Delhi, 1999.

Jaffer, Mehru, *The Book of Muhammad,* Penguin Books India Ltd., New Delhi, 2012.

Jafri, S.H.M., *The Origins and Early Development of Shi'a Islam*, Oxford University Press, Karachi, Pakistan, 2000.

Jarret, H.S., *Jalaluddin A's Suyuti's History of the Caliphs,* Kitab Bhavan, New Delhi, 2010.

Kahf, Monzar, *Al-nusus,* King Abdul Aziz University, Jeddah, 1990.

Khaldun Ibn, *Muqaddimah,* English translation by Franz Rosenthal, Princeton University Press, Princeton, 1970.

Khan, Arshi, "Islam, Tolerance and Pluralism", *Indian Journal of Secularism,* Vol. 16, No. 1, April-June, 2012, pp. 50-90.

Khursheed Ahmad (ed.), *First International Conference on Islamic Economics: Selected Papers*, Amar Prakashan, Delhi, 1984.

Kidwai, Abdur Raheem, *365 Sayings of Prophet Muhammad,* Jaico Publishing House, Mumbai, Sixth Impression, 2012.

Madrasi, Abdul Khaliq, *Ashab-e-Sufa* (Urdu Edition), Maktab Islamia, Delhi, 2007.

Masudul Hasan, *Hazart Ali Murtuda*, Aakif Book Depot,

Delhi.

Masudul Hassan, *Hadrat Othman Ghani,* Kitab Bhavan, New Delhi, 1999.

Momin. A.R., *Islam and Pluralism,* Jamia Hamdard, New Delhi, 2004.

Momin, A.R., *The Relevance of Prophet Muhammad's Life and Teachings in an Insecure and Fragile World,* Institute of Objective Studies, New Delhi, 2010.

Moududi, S.A.A., *Khilafat wa Malukiat,* Markazi Makatab-e-Islami Publishers, New Delhi, 2008.

Nabhani, Taqiuddin, *The Economic System in Islam,* Milli Publications, New Delhi, 2002.

—*The Social Security in Islam,* Milli Publications, New Delhi, 2002.

—*The Islamic State,* Milli Publications, New Delhi, 2002.

Nadwi, Sayed Abul Hasan Ali, *Al-Murtuza*, Academy of Islamic Research and Publications, Lucknow, 3rd Edition, 1991. The present author has followed its English translation entitled *The Life of Caliph Ali.* It was rendered into English by S. Mohiuddin Ahmed and published by Academy of Islamic Research and Publications, Lucknow, 1991.

Nadvi, Shah Moinuddin, *Hazrat Ali Al Murtuza*, Idara Isha'at –e-Diniyat (P) Ltd., New Delhi, 1997.

Nizami, Khaliq Ahmad, *Some Aspects of Religion and Politics in India During Thirteenth Century,* Idarah-i-Adbiyat-i-Dilli, Delhi, 1974.

Palmer Monte and Princess Palmer, *Islamic Extremism,* Foundation Books, New Delhi, 2011.

Peerzade, Sayed Afzal, *Islamic Public Finance and Policy,* Idarah-e-Adbiyat-e-Dilli, Delhi, 2004.

—*On Taxation in Islam,* Idarah-i- Adbiyat-e-Dilli, Delhi, 2009.

—"A Note on Economic Ideas of Caliph Ali With Special Reference to His Letter to Malik al-Ashtar", *Journal of Social Sciences and Humanities,* Islamia University of

Bahawalpur, Pakistan, Vol. 8. No. 2, 2010.

—"Quranic Perspective of Compensation Principle, *Economic Problems and The Teachings of Quran,* Idarah Uloom al-Quran, Shibli Bagh, Aligarh, 2011.

—"Ali, the Caliph: His Poor Subjects and Pro-Poor Government", *Indian Journal of Politics,* Vol. 45, Nos. 3-4, 2012.

Rahman, Afzal-ur, *Economic Doctrines of Islam,* Vol. I, Islamic Publication Ltd., Lahore, 1980,

Rao, M.G. and Mihir Rakshit (eds.) *Public Economics: Theory and Practice-Essays in Honour of Amaresh Bagchi*, Sage India, 2011.

Razi, Muhammad and M.H.Syed, *Ali: The Lion of Almighty*, Anmol Publications Pvt. Ltd., New Delhi, 2009.

Siddiqui, Muhammad Nejatullah, "Muslims Economics Thinking: A Survey of Contemporary Literature" in Khursheed Ahmad (ed.), *First International Conference on Islamic Economics: Selected Papers*, Amar Prakashan, Delhi, 1984.

Shaban, Sabry S., *A Classified Bibliography of Islamic Economics,* Part I-III, Islamic Research Foundation of Astan-e-Quds Razvi, Islamic Economics Department, Mashad, Iran, 1989.

Shah, Waliullah Muhadith Dehlvi, *al-Budur al-Bazigah,* Kitab Bhavan, New Delhi, 1997.

Shah, Waliullah Muhadith Dehlvi, *Izalatul Khulfa* (Urdu edition in two volumes), Maktab-e-Hafizi, Deoband, undated.

Shaik Ali Muttaqi Hindi Burhanpuri, *Kanz al-ummal* (Urdu) Idarah-e-Isha'at-e-Islam, Deoband, India, 2010.

Sherwani, Haroon Khan, *Muslim Political Thought and Administration*, Munshi Ram Manoharlal Publishers Pvt. Ltd., 1981.

Sherwani, Muhammad Habibur Rahman Khan, *Life of Abu Bakr: The First Caliph of Islam,* (3rd Edition), Adam Publishers and Distributors, Delhi.

Shibli Numani, *Al-Farooq,* Naaz Book Depot, Delhi.

Suyuti, Jalaluddin, *Tarikh al Khulfa,* (Urdu), Farid Book Depot, Pvt. Ltd., Delhi, 2004.

Werner, Ende and Udo Steinback, *Islam in the World Today: A Handbook of Politics, Religion, Culture and Society*, Cornell University Press, Cornell, 2005.

Zaim, Sasahuddin, "Contemporary Turkish Literature on Islamic Economics", in Khursheed Ahmad (ed.), *First International Conference on Islamic Economics: Selected Papers*, Amar Prakashan, Delhi, 1984.

Zallum, Adul Qadeem, *How the Khilafah Was Destroyed,* Milli Publications, New Delhi, 2002.

—*Funds in the Khilafah State,* Milli Publications, New Delhi, 2002.

Zayadan, Jurji, *History of Islamic Civilisation: Umayyads and Abbasids*, translated into English by D.S. Margoliouth, Kitab Bhavan, 2006.

Index

Index